Voices in the Dark

Voices in the Dark

My Life as a Medium

Leslie Flint

Macmillan

© Doreen Montgomery and Leslie Flint 1971

SBN 333 12201 1

First published 1971
MACMILLAN LONDON LTD
London and Basingstoke
Associated companies in New York Toronto
Dublin Melbourne Johannesburg and Madras

Printed in Great Britain by
RICHARD CLAY (THE CHAUCER PRESS), LTD
Bungay, Suffolk

FOR
ROSIE *and* BRAM

Illustrations

Acknowledgements

THE credit for this book should go to Doreen Montgomery for encouraging me to tell my story. No one could have had a kinder or more expert editor.

My grateful thanks are also due to Maurice Barbanell, the editor of *Two Worlds* and *Psychic News*, and his staff who gave me so much help with my research for this book.

One

In spite of a childhood which would give any modern child-psychiatrist nightmares, or perhaps because of it, I have reached the age of fifty-nine without falling prey to neurosis, psychosis or even the screaming meemies. I am a happy man. I have friends who delight me, hobbies to absorb me and I find satisfaction and fulfilment in my work. I do my work by sitting wide awake in total darkness with other people.

I am a medium. I have the rare gift known as the independent direct voice. I do not speak in trance, I need no trumpets or other paraphernalia. The voices of the dead speak directly to their friends or relatives and are located in space a little above my head and slightly to one side of me. They are objective voices which my sitters can record on their own tape-recorders to play later in the privacy of their homes. Sometimes those who speak from beyond the grave achieve only a whisper, hoarse and strained, at other times they speak clearly and fluently in voices recognisably their own during life, and even after thirty-five years of my mediumship I do not fully understand what are the conditions which cause the phenomena to vary in this way. I do know I have learned more about life and people and human problems and emotions by sitting in the dark than I could possibly have learned in any other way, and those who have taught me the most are people who, dead to this world, are living in the next.

It seems to me that having entered my sixtieth year, it is

9

time to set down on paper the story of my strange talent and the life it has led me, and where better to begin than at the beginning.

My mother was much too beautiful for her own good and she loved pleasure and admiration, so no one in the dingy street where she lived with her widowed mother in St Albans was very surprised when she left her job in a local factory and disappeared from her usual haunts. No doubt they charitably assumed the worst and in this case they were perfectly right, and I was born in a Salvation Army Home in Hackney. My mother refused to have me adopted and, with a great deal more courage than she would need in the same circumstances today went home to St Albans with her inconvenient bundle to face the neighbours' music. But Fate with a lot of help from my grandmother had been working at her loom as the saying goes and grandmother and Fate between them came up with a pretty disastrous pattern. Instead of the recriminations and ostracism my mother expected she found my father waiting with an offer of marriage and a home in a furnished room. Forthwith my arrival into the world was made legal, official and reasonably respectable.

Their marriage was doomed from the beginning. They were pitifully young, desperately poor, and they had been coerced into maturity by their elders long before they were ready for it. My mother who loved gaiety and bright lights, pretty clothes and the admiration of men found herself trapped in a seedy room with a baby who cried endlessly and a husband who drank most of his wages and put the rest on horses which never seemed to win. But somehow they survived three years of discord, fighting each other every inch of the way until the 1914–18 war broke out when I was three years old. My father was one of the first men in St Albans to volunteer for the army, not I imagine from any fervent patriotism, but simply to get away from the domestic hell he lived in. My mother accepted her husband's departure for France with composure and, having arranged with her mother to take care of me during the day, she got a job in a local factory making munitions and life began again for her. She had her army allotment, she was earning money in the factory and St Albans was full of men on leave, about to return to the trenches, who were only too pleased to take my pretty mother out and about and give her the gaiety she craved.

One of my very early memories, vivid to this day, is of waking up in the dark to find I was alone in the room which was our home and of feeling scared and lonely and desperately frightened that my mother had gone away like my father had gone and neither of them would ever come back. Somehow I dressed myself in the dark and wandered out of the house. I still remember standing in the pitch-dark street in the rain, calling and calling for my mother, but there was no one to listen and I sat down on a neighbour's doorstep and fell asleep. When my mother eventually came home she found me sitting in front of their fire drinking hot milk. When she got me back to our room she spanked me soundly for showing her up in front of the people next door.

As it turned out that night of desolation was the prelude to a period of bliss. My mother realised she could not again leave me alone in our room while she went out enjoying herself without inviting interference from the neighbours. She had no intention however of giving up her freedom and so she concocted a plan. Every evening as soon as she was dressed to go out she would take me by the hand to the local cinema where she would hand me over to Mrs Knight, the wife of the manager, who for three or four pence would put me in a seat where she could keep an eye on me and there I would stay until the cinema closed and my mother came to collect me. I was not old enough to take in a great deal of the many films I saw but those nights at the pictures delighted me. I loved the thrill which rippled through the audience as the lights went out, the excited feeling that something wonderful was about to happen. When the film actually started, rustling and fidgeting would abruptly stop and all eyes were glued to the flickering figures on the screen. I loved the 'mood music' which the pianist played on the upright piano. I came to recognise love music, angry music and the exciting hurry-hurry music when the hero or his sweetheart were in some dire predicament. I loved every minute of these nights at the cinema. But this halcyon interlude came to an abrupt end when my mother eloped with one of her admirers and disappeared from my life. I was collected from our room by my grandmother and taken to live with her in her two-down two-up cottage in the poor street of terrace houses where she existed rather than lived on a few shillings a week. The cost of feeding an extra mouth was really beyond her, but my grandmother knew her duty when she saw it, and even if it meant cutting her own living to the bare bone she was determined to do her duty by her abandoned grandson.

My grandmother could not read or write and she had strong principles which she inculcated into me with a leathery hand if she thought it necessary. She worked very hard and I never knew her to sit still. She would spend the whole day at the big tub in the kitchen doing not only our own washing but laundry she took in from the neighbours to earn a few extra pence. If the weather were fine Gran would hang the washing in the yard to dry but in the winter months every Monday morning she would string lines across the kitchen which was also our living-room and damp sheets, shirts and towels flapped in our faces for two days until they were dry enough to be pressed with the heavy flat-iron. The extra pence she earned in this way helped to support us. We also had a lodger who paid a few shillings for his bed and board and without his contribution to our budget I doubt if we could have existed at all. I suppose it is hard for members of our affluent society to imagine poverty as wretched as ours, but in those days a grown man might earn a wage of 12s 6d for a week's work and a married man might bring up his family on a pound a week.

Gran and I had occasional luxuries. I remember being

given four pennies to run to the corner shop to buy twopence worth of broken biscuits and twopence worth of jam. Coal was a luxury often out of reach and in the autumn Gran would borrow a battered old pram from a neighbour and we would go 'wooding' in the countryside round St Albans and collect fuel to store for the winter. We spent many afternoons doing this because our old terrace cottage was cold and damp in winter and we had no money for illness. I can see my grandmother now sitting by a wood fire backed up with soot from the chimney to make it last longer, mending, patching and darning, and myself sitting at her feet revelling in the warmth of the fire. Even if the clothes we wore were old and shabby, mended and patched, they were always clean and cared-for and respectable. Respectability was terribly important to the working class in those days and when Gran went out, though her clothes were even then old-fashioned, indeed they were Victorian in style, she always looked neat and tidy.

My grandmother had enormous influence on me and since she had a strict moral and ethical code I was brought up according to her own high ideals of what was right and what was wrong, though without any formal religious observance because Gran would have thought it disrespectful to enter God's house in her shabby clothes and she was self-conscious about her illiteracy which made it impossible for her to follow the service. But when I was small she sent me to Sunday school and I wore a Sunday suit and a clean collar and my face was scrubbed and my hair brushed flat with water. The Sunday suit would be returned the next morning to the pawnshop where it remained most of the week in return for a couple of shillings to buy food but at the Sunday school I was clean, neat and respectable. I liked Sunday school, especially in the winter months because it was warm and I enjoyed listening to the Bible stories and learning about heaven and hell and how dead people would rise from their graves to be judged when the Angel Gabriel blew his silver trumpet on the Last Day, and I accepted all I heard as the literal truth. One day I dis-

13

covered that a small boy in the class attended three Sunday schools and this intrigued me. Did they all have different gods? What kind of stories did the other teachers tell? But it was simpler than that. By attending three Sunday schools this enterprising child qualified for three Christmas Treats. Now the Christmas Treat was the biggest and most thrilling event in my whole year. There was a Christmas tree decorated in what to me was a breathtakingly beautiful fashion and every child got a toy from its laden branches. Then there was a magic lantern show followed by a glorious feast of jam sandwiches, iced buns and cakes, with lemonade to drink. Finally, when we went home we were presented with an orange and a balloon. I thought the boy was terribly clever to achieve three such brilliant occasions in one year. Timidly, I asked if I could copy, and graciously he said I might. And so for a whole year, unknown to Gran, my friend and I went to three different Sunday schools on alternate Sundays and duly earned three Christmas Treats. Privately gloating over three toys, three oranges, three balloons, not to mention the memory of three blow-outs, I felt vaguely sinful but quite determined to repeat the manoeuvre the following year.

It was about this time, in the summer of 1918, that I had what I know now to be my first psychic experience. I vividly remember being in our kitchen with Gran when my Aunt Nell came in and flopped into a chair, crying. Her husband had been killed in France and she was followed into the kitchen by a soldier carrying a kitbag containing Uncle Alf's possessions. But behind the soldier with the kitbag walked another soldier who stood in our kitchen looking lost and sad and pulling at Aunt Nell's sleeve, trying to attract her attention. Aunt Nell took no notice of him at all and shortly he just vanished. Later when Aunt Nell showed me a photograph of Uncle Alf I recognised him as the sad-looking soldier who was trying to make Aunt Nell pay attention to him, but when I told her about it both she and my grandmother were angry with me for telling lies. When I persisted in saying it

14

was the truth I got a good clout from Gran.

Another time, as I came in from school I heard voices from the kitchen, Gran's voice and that of a woman unknown to me. When I went into the kitchen my grandmother was not talking at all, she was sitting in her wicker chair sewing, but standing at her side was an elderly woman with a large mole on her chin who vanished as I came into the room. When I asked Gran what had happened to the lady who had been talking to her she told me I was imagining things, she had been quite alone all afternoon. I described the woman I had seen and when I mentioned the mole on her chin I got clouted again because, 'It's Mrs Pugh you're talking about and she has been dead and buried for a month or more.' After that episode I learned to keep quiet about the people I saw who vanished so abruptly.

I was not one of the giant intellects at school, but in one subject I shone quite brightly and this was Art. I loved drawing and painting and I liked Mr Lewis, the Art teacher. He was a tall gaunt man, I suppose in his late forties, and he had been badly gassed in the trenches so that he coughed continually with a hard hacking sound. Mr Lewis used to praise my efforts and encourage me to aspire to an Art School training when I was older. Even then I knew we were too poor for this to be anything but an impossible dream, but his encouragement and praise meant a great deal to me and I remember the red-letter days when we would pin up my work for the rest of the school to admire. Eventually, I suppose, I came to look on him as a kind of father figure in my life probably because my own father had remained in it so briefly. I can remember to this day the grief and shock I felt when Mr Lewis died after an illness lasting a few days. It was some small comfort to learn that he was to be honoured by a military funeral because his death was due to his service in the trenches, and twelve boys from the school were going to be chosen to follow the coffin draped with the Union Jack. As I had been one of his best pupils and he had taken so much interest in my work it simply did not occur to me that I would not be chosen to follow his coffin to the cemetery, but I was passed over and my grief for his death was made the more bitter.

When I was twelve I found a job I could do in the mornings before I went to school. It was in a house in what I thought of as the posh part of St Albans. It was a well furnished house and they had carpets so I thought they must be very rich. I got up at six every morning and walked to work whistling happily at the thought of actually earning money and for an hour and a half I cleaned the grates and lit the fires and did other domestic chores, then I hurried home and gobbled down whatever was on offer for breakfast, usually bread and margarine and tea, and went off to school. Then my grandmother qualified for her old age pension of 10s a week and while our finances took on a brighter hue, every Friday morning became a nightmare for me. Gran could only draw her pension on Friday and by that time in the week she was penniless and she had to have it in the morning to buy food for the week-end. Now, because she could not write her name she would make a cross on her pension form and an arrangement was made with the postmaster of the sub-post office across the road from our house whereby he honoured her cross and handed her 10s to me. But the post office did not open until nine o'clock, at which time I was due in school, so every Friday morning I had to hang about outside the post office waiting for the postmaster to open up and give me the 10s, knowing with every minute which passed I was going to be late for school again. As soon as I got the 10s I would rush across the road and give Gran the money then I would run all the way to school. But every Friday morning without fail I was late for class and, since Gran could not write an excuse for me, as often as not I was caned. In fact it became a ritual. At nine-thirty every Friday I was knocking timidly on the door of the headmaster's study and at twenty-five to ten I was being caned. I was not the bravest boy in the school, but however hard the headmaster laid into me with the cane on a Friday morning I never let out the smallest whimper and all because of a picture hanging on the wall of his study. It was a painting of Queen Boadicea in her chariot and for some reason it gave me courage. I felt Boadicea and I had something in common and I must be as brave as she had been to be worthy of her. When I stood outside the headmaster's door on a Friday morning it comforted me to think I would see her again even if it meant I was going to be caned. I would try to be caned on the hand rather than on the bottom even though it hurt more so I could stand facing her picture while the headmaster wielded the stick.

For a long time I believed my picture was the real Queen Boadicea and when I learned it was an impostor I was shattered. Some years before I was born St Albans had staged a pageant of its history and one of the set pieces in it had been the uprising of Boadicea against the Romans. My picture was a portrait of the woman who had played the part of my heroine and she had been chosen for the role because she was the wife of the local milkman and thus able to commandeer the milk-float for her chariot. As soon as I knew the absurd truth the picture lost its magic and when the headmaster laid into me with the cane I wept. It simply did not occur to me to tell my grandmother about these weekly beatings. In those days children had not the habit of complaining nor had their elders the habit of listening to them if they did. One of the maxims dinned into me as a child was 'what can't be cured must be endured'.

My grandmother was a wonderful woman. She gave me all she could from the little she had but her life was too harsh, the daily struggle for a bare existence too grim, too unrelenting for tenderness between us.

Our improved finances now made it possible for Gran and me to taste pleasure. For threepence or fourpence each we would go to the local cinema and escape for a couple of hours into an enchanted world where all the women were beautiful and the men were godlike.

The films we saw were silent films and I would read out the sub-titles to my grandmother. Perhaps the absence of the spoken word stimulated imagination more strongly but audiences in those days identified wholly and completely with the stars they idolised and they watched their films as if they were seeing real people living real lives. How we rejoiced or suffered with the heroine, how we urged on the hero or warned him of the machinations of the villain usually greeted with hisses. In the hungry twenties the working class was neither as sophisticated nor as educated as its modern counterpart, millions could not read or write and lived in squalid poverty. The cinema brought romance, glamour and excitement into their lives and even if the intellectuals called it the opium of the masses at least it was a relatively harmless drug and retailed at a price even the poorest could afford occasionally. My grandmother and I saw all the great stars and 'the pictures' were our delight and joy. At least once a week we would buy fourpenny tickets to our enchanted world and sit, eyes glued to the screen, transported. We followed the serial and if at the end of an episode Pearl White was left bound hand and foot in the path of an express train we could hardly wait for the next episode to see if she would be saved. Deep down we knew very well she was bound to be rescued but that did not stop us from living on tenterhooks for a week.

About this time St Albans got its first super-cinema and there was to be a gala opening with *The Four Horsemen of the Apocalypse* starring Rudolph Valentino. Seats for this glamorous event were expensive and anyway they were all taken by the rich and privileged folk of the town, but at the last moment we heard that a few cheap seats would be available for those who queued on the great night. Naturally Gran and I arrived at the cinema hours before time and queued for these precious seats. We stood in line for three hours while the long queue shuffled forward inch by inch but at last we got inside and sat down triumphantly in two plush seats in the very front row of the auditorium. The long wait and the seats which cricked our necks and made our eyes ache because they were too near the screen did not matter a jot to us once the film started. We adored every minute of it and we thought Rudolph Valentino was the most marvellous actor we had ever seen. From then on we were his devoted fans.

The sub-post office across the street from us was a kind of forum for the exchange of news, gossip and above all information about jobs, especially about jobs. Those were days when work was pitifully scarce, for every vacancy there were literally dozens of applicants and even the rumour of work was enough to send desperate men trudging miles in the hope of being taken on at any wage, under any conditions just so they could feed their families and regain their self-respect. One day not long after my thirteenth birthday the postmaster in the sub-post office across the street told me the local cemetery wanted a strong willing lad to work as assistant to the gardeners; though I was hardly carried away by the thought of working among graves, I made up my mind to try for the job and if I got it I would leave school and begin my working life. I did get it and so my formal education came to an end and I started work in the cemetery at 12s 6d a week.

My work consisted of keeping graves neat and tidy, clipping grass verges, weeding and rolling gravel paths with a heavy iron roller. I also helped to dig new graves and after the funeral to fill them in again. It was hard back-breaking labour but it was a job. I was earning my keep.

I remember one cold blustery day in winter when I was working on my graves clipping the grass verges while we waited for a hearse to arrive with a funeral party. We, that is the other gardeners and I, had been busy all morning digging the grave for this burial and after some months of working in the cemetery I knew from experience that the length of the funeral service would depend on the age of the clergyman who turned up with the hearse. A young keen curate would be likely to ignore the cutting wind and the rain and conduct the service in a reverent unhurried way, but an elderly parson would rattle through as quickly as he could to get out of the cold and back to his fireside. I was hoping like mad for an old man and a quick farewell to the departed. My luck was in and the aged clergyman who turned up with the cortège rattled through the proceedings like one o'clock and was off like a shot. After the mourners had gone we began to fill in the new grave, a deep one intended in due course to hold three coffins. Our first task was to withdraw the cords which had lowered the coffin into the grave but on this occasion one of the cords had stuck and we couldn't shift it for all our tugging. So, since I was the youngest, the smallest and the lightest of all the cemetery gardeners I had to climb down a ladder into the grave and stand on the lid of the coffin so newly placed in it to help to free the cord. I must confess the task distressed me but it was part of my job and I had to do it. Maybe I did it too well for from that day on whenever a coffin got jammed or a cord trapped invariably I was the unfortunate junior who was summoned to perform this horrid operation. There were other chores in the cemetery which I found distasteful, even frightening, such as the times when an unusual number of people died in winter or during an epidemic and we would be so busy during the day we had to fill in the new graves at night by the flickering light of lanterns. I found this eerie and melancholy work, even more so on the occasions when I had to get down into a grave to perform my hated speciality of disentangling coffin cords.

I was fifteen in the summer of 1926 and I was beginning to wonder whether, if I learned all I could from the senior gardeners about the care of plants and flowers, I might one day escape from the sadness of the cemetery to work in the grounds of some gentleman's country mansion. Pursuing this ambition I made myself very unpopular badgering the gardeners for information about their work and following them about while they did it.

One hot August day that year the world learned with stunned disbelief that Rudolph Valentino had died suddenly in New York at the age of thirty-one. Millions had adored this man and the wave of shock and grief seemed to travel right round the globe. In my small corner, I also grieved for his death and found the world a sadder place because of it. How could I guess that far in the future I would be more friendly with Valentino dead than I could ever have been had he lived?

Two

TACTFULLY out of sight behind a yew hedge in the cemetery was a potting-shed where the gardeners ate their sandwiches, brewed tea and talked during the midday break. Mr Hobbs, my immediate boss, enjoyed laying down the law on any and every subject and it was his voice, gritty as a gravel path, which dominated these sessions. He was a lean weathered man with a habit of shaking his bony forefinger, deeply stained by nicotine, at whoever he harangued. He was supposed to be a great reader which gave him an edge in argument as invariably he quoted some book he claimed to have read to contradict any opinion but his own. As the rest of us read only sports results or, in my case, magazines about the stars and their doings in Hollywood, Mr Hobbs had become something of an oracle.

Once a mild little man called Carter was telling us about his conversion at a Salvation Army meeting and I could not help being struck by the way his face lit up when he spoke of the joy he felt when he knew he was saved. But Mr Hobbs would have none of it. He shook his bony finger in Mr Carter's face and grated scornfully, 'You want to read your Darwin, man. He showed up that rubbish for a pack of lies years ago.' Clearly Mr Carter had never heard of his Darwin and, nothing loth, Mr Hobbs expounded his version of the theory of natural selection. But Mr Carter refused to be blinded by science. 'I happen to believe if we live decent lives here below we shall go to our reward in the hereafter,' he said stoutly. Mr Hobbs got quite worked up.

'Haven't I just been telling you there isn't any hereafter! It's all evolution. First we was fish, then we was apes and now we are human beings and when we kick the bucket we'll be compost for the roses in some graveyard and that is absolutely all there is to it.'

I was the youngest of the gardeners and shy about butting in on my elders' talk but I hated to see the light go out in little Mr Carter's face and timidly I tried to support him by telling about the time I saw Uncle Alf in our kitchen after he was killed. Mr Hobbs snorted. 'It was in your mind, boy! You was thinking about the deceased and you imagined you saw him. Hypnotised yourself into it most likely.' Made bold by a grateful look from Mr Carter, I persisted.

'I never saw Uncle Alf in my whole life so how could I imagine him? I didn't even know who he was until Aunt Nell showed me the snapshot she found in his kitbag.'

Mr Hobbs fixed me with his washed-out blue eyes, tapped his forehead with the bony finger. 'Take my tip, young feller-me-lad, don't you go telling them tales to anyone in the medical profession or you'll find yourself inside Shenley Asylum before you're very much older.' The eyes and the finger were too much for me.

'No, Mr Hobbs,' I said meekly.

At seventeen I had been concerned with life, with earning my living, growing up, enjoying such pleasures as came my way, and I had not given much thought to the question of life after death, but the incident in the potting-shed made me think seriously about such matters for the first time. Admittedly, working in the cemetery gave me the impression death was a pretty final event. When the mourners had gone and the earth was filled in and pressed down on the new grave I knew very well the corpse underneath had already begun to decompose, and the resurrection when Gabriel blew his silver trumpet on the last day seemed an impossible lie. Was Mr

23

Hobbs right? Were we just apes who had learned to be smarter than our forebears who lived in trees? Was our universe a cosmic accident doomed eventually to total extinction? What then was the conviction which gave timid Mr Carter his inner glow and gave him the courage to stand up to the formidable Mr Hobbs? I thought about seeing Uncle Alf and Mrs Pugh when I was a child. They had not struck me at the time as being anything but ordinary living people yet they were dead and Mrs Pugh's body, at least, must have been far advanced in decay. Had I really seen them or was I heading for the asylum, as Mr Hobbs seemed to think? For days on end I pondered these and other questions, wondering where I could go, whom I could find to give me the answers. It began to seem to me that the most important thing in life was to know the meaning of death.

I started to haunt the local churches. Every week I went from one to another hoping to find some clue, some grain of truth in which I could believe, but like Omar, I 'heard great argument but evermore came out by the same door as in I went.' I wanted so much more than the Churches could offer. I was not content 'to have faith in' or 'to hope for', I wanted to know, I needed some conviction on which to build my life. If death meant oblivion I could accept that, even without regret, but I wanted to be certain. If there was a life after death I wanted proof of it and I wanted to know what kind of life it would be. After many weeks of earnest seeking in the various denominations of the Christian Church I had found neither conviction nor any hope of it and I was beginning to despair.

I read a notice in the local library about a meeting of the Theosophical Society, someone was going to address them on The Ancient Wisdom. This seemed right up my street, for what was I looking for if it were not wisdom? I borrowed a dictionary from the library to look up 'theosophical' and I was thrilled to read 'theosophy' was 'immediate divine illumination claimed to be possessed by specially gifted persons'.

I could hardly wait for the night of that meeting.

There were very few people in the audience on the big night and I felt sorry for the speaker who had come from London for the occasion, so when he stepped on to the rostrum I kept on clapping long after everyone else had stopped, to make him feel welcome. He spoke in what I thought of as a haw-haw voice and used words I had never heard before so I thought he must be very educated and as he was also specially gifted according to Chambers' dictionary, I prepared to drink in his every word. Unfortunately most of his discourse passed right over my devoted head. He had a lot to say about Astral Bodies but he did not bother to explain what they were. Things looked up when he began to talk about souls who had progressed spiritually on the other side who would sometimes reincarnate again in earthly bodies to perform some special work. This seemed hopeful. At least this educated, specially gifted man was taking it for granted there *was* another side. Then came a real shot in the arm. The speaker solemnly warned the audience to have nothing to do with Spiritualist mediums who, when they got in touch with the dead, contacted only entities who were unevolved and hanging about the earth and the low vibrations they brought with them were not helpful. This was the first time I had ever heard it was possible to get in touch with the dead and I was thrilled at the very idea. If it were true then whatever kind of entity one contacted, high vibrations or low, it would surely prove there was life after death, or so at any rate I reasoned at the time.

Obviously my next step was to find these Spiritualists with their low vibrations, whatever that meant, and see what I could learn from them. I kept asking people where I could find them but no one seemed to know. Sometimes the people I asked acted strangely. They turned on a heel and stalked away looking affronted or they screwed a finger into a temple and gave me a pitying look. I began to think I was trailing some sinister secret society. Spiritualism today is respectably and officially a religion with some three million adherents in this country, but in those days mediums still risked prosecution under the Witchcraft Act of 1735 and to a certain extent they were driven underground. I did not know this at the time, of course, and I concluded I had reached another dead end.

Some weeks after I had more or less given up the search for the elusive Spiritualists, I had been given the task of tidying up a row of graves known as Contracts because relatives paid the cemetery a fixed sum every year for their upkeep. When I had finished them I noticed a neglected, overgrown grave beyond them. I felt sad for this unknown for whom no one seemed to care and decided I had time enough before the midday break to tidy him up. I was busy clipping away the long grass and weeds on this forlorn grave when a woman walked up the path carrying a sheaf of fresh flowers. She removed flowers from the grave she was visiting which, to my uncritical eye, seemed almost fresh. She threw these in a refuse bin and put her fresh sheaf on the grave and went away. By this time my efforts had uncovered the name on the headstone of the sad grave I was working on and I saw the man buried there had once been known as Edwin Lewis. With a shock of recognition I studied the dates on the headstone and I was left in no doubt that this was the grave of my dear Mr Lewis, the teacher who had believed I might one day become an artist. The grave was as spick and span as I could make it so I retrieved the woman's almost-new flowers from the bin, shook them out and tidied them up as best I could, put them into a jam-jar and placed them on Mr Lewis' grave with a small prayer for his happiness wherever he might be.

. As I sat in a corner of the potting-shed eating my midday snack, I could hear Mr Hobbs' voice rasping above the rest as usual. 'And so I said to the missus, I said, it's a lot of bloody nonsense. I've been burying stiffs for thirty years, I said, and believe me, they stay buried. How can they come back? Them Spiritualists are after your money, you silly cow!' I almost choked on my fish-paste sandwich. Mr Hobbs grated on. '"What's more," I said, "if you set foot in the Friends' Meeting **Place** this night to try calling up the departed, your hat with the grapes on goes into the back of the fire." '

Sympathy for Mrs Hobbs was drowned by excitement. At last I had a clue to these elusive Spiritualists. Come what may, I would be at the Quakers' hall that night.

Scrubbed and wearing my Sunday suit I arrived at the Friends' Meeting-house and read a hand-written notice outside which said there would be a Spiritualist service that evening with Mrs Annie Johnson, the well-known trance medium, giving an address followed by clairvoyance. Trance? Clairvoyance? Well, there was only one way to find out. I went inside.

The hall was only half-filled and I decided to sit in the back row as near an exit as I could get in case I wanted to beat a hasty retreat before the proceedings were over. Gradually the hall filled up and hymn books were handed round. On the cover of mine I read *The Greater World Christian Spiritualist Hymn Book*. Ah! I thought, so they are Christians, are they? But, looking about me, I didn't think there was much of a church atmosphere about this bare hall. People were chatting, even laughing together, there were none of the church ornaments which I had been accustomed to admire during my months of perambulation round other Christian churches in search of truth. When the service started I was even less impressed. It seemed a haphazard business. I considered it lacked the professional touch. In fact, I felt somewhat superior to these simple folk who sang hymns I did not know to a wheezy old harmonium and who prayed in an almost chatty way as if they were talking to the Almighty on friendly terms. It seemed presumptuous to me. This is the worst service I've been to yet, I thought.

Suddenly there was a stir and a rustle among the congregation as a man and a woman walked together down the aisle to the platform at the other end of the hall. They sat down on two straight-backed chairs facing us.

The man was small, drooping, elderly, he reminded me

27

irresistibly of pictures I had seen of the notorious Dr Crippen who had chopped up his wife and eloped with his typist before I was born.

The woman was imposingly dressed in purple with a large silver pectoral cross. I approved of the cross, it gave a touch of authenticity to the proceedings. Dr Crippen got to his feet and said one of the chatty prayers, then he invited us to sing another hymn. During the singing I observed my purple lady dropping off to sleep. After the hymn, Dr Crippen announced that Mrs Annie Johnson would now give her trance address. So my purple lady was the medium, but didn't silly little Dr Crippen know she had fallen asleep? To my astonishment the sleeping woman stood up and began to speak. I sat up with a jerk at the first words, for booming through the hall there came from the lips of this sleeping woman a voice no lady had any right to have, a deep, resonant, cultured voice unmistakably male. Could it possibly be a man dressed up as a woman, I wondered? Would anyone dare to do such a thing in a Christian church? But no one in my vicinity seemed perturbed or even surprised, they were listening intently to what was being said, so I stopped worrying about it and paid attention. The talk was about Life Eternal. The man's voice coming through the lips of Mrs Johnson said he loved to come back to earth to comfort those who were grieving for the physical loss of their loved ones, to assure them the dear ones were only lost to human sight, they were still living, still loving those left behind them, and from the happier world where they now were they could sometimes send messages of love and hope to those on earth, and tonight he was going to help some of those who had gone before to give messages to their friends present in the hall. To put it mildly, I was staggered. Was this woman, or was she a man, proposing to call up the dead? I remembered the warnings of the theosophist man about dangers of low vibrations, and wondered if I should leave before this part of the programme. But in for a penny, in for a pound I told myself and sat tight.

The medium sat down and Dr Crippen invited us to sing a hymn called 'Silently now, we wait for Thee'. During the singing I wondered just what they were waiting for and had I been wise to decide to remain, but I did not want to push past the row of women between me and the exit, so more from shyness than conviction I stayed and sang with the rest.

The hymn ended and we all sat down. Mrs Johnson walked to the edge of the platform and pointed to a woman near the front of the congregation and began to talk to her in a quiet pleasantly feminine voice totally unlike the one she had used when she was asleep. She told the woman her husband was standing beside her and he was anxious for the woman to know he no longer had the terrible pain in his chest from which he suffered before he passed away. Mrs Johnson described the husband even down to the colour of his suit and a club tie she said he was wearing. The woman accepted what she said with an emphatic nodding of her head. I strained my eyes trying to see this man Mrs Johnson said was standing beside the woman but I could see neither hide nor hair of him and I concluded it was some kind of act cooked up by the pair of them which did not impress me. There were other messages of a similar nature for other people in the hall and one or two of these people grew very emotional as they accepted what Mrs Johnson told them as true. I was still convinced that Mrs Johnson was working with accomplices planted in the congregation.

'I want to speak to the young man in the back row,' said Mrs Johnson suddenly and pointed straight at me. I was petrified at being singled out and looked round hopefully to see if there were some other young man she might mean, but I was the only male in the whole row of seats and the finger continued to point at me. 'Put up your hand, young man,' said Mrs Johnson at last, and very nervously I raised my arm. 'Yes,' she said, 'I mean you. There is a man here who wants to thank you for the flowers you put on his grave this morning. He tells me he was a schoolmaster and his name was Edwin

Lewis. Do you understand this?' I was flabbergasted, but Mrs Johnson was not finished with me. She went on to give an accurate description of Mr Lewis as I remembered him and said he was interested in my drawing and painting when he was on earth. 'He was given a military funeral,' she added casually. By this time I was very hot under the collar. How could this woman whom I had never seen in my life, who could not possibly know anything about me tell me about a man I had known in my childhood and describe what I had done that morning when I was entirely alone at Mr Lewis' grave? But Mrs Johnson was not done with me even yet. She described other people she said she could see round me including an Arab. What was an Arab doing around me I wondered, what did he want with me? He was a Guide, said Mrs Johnson, and he was not really an Arab, he was someone who dressed as an Arab. This seemed to me to get more involved by the minute. When Mrs Johnson finally told me this young Arab, who wasn't an Arab, wanted me to develop as a medium to be of service to humanity, I thought she was well off the mark. 'In the not too distant future,' Mrs Johnson insisted, 'you will be doing the same kind of work as I am doing and you will become a very famous medium.' This seemed so crazy and so impossible I shrugged it off and crept out of the hall as unobtrusively as I could.

For a long time before I slept that night I turned these events over and over and over again in my mind and the more I thought about what Mrs Johnson had told me the more fantastic it seemed. I could no longer believe it was a trick played with the help of people planted in the congregation because it had happened to me, and no one but I could have known what I had done when I was entirely alone, with not another soul in sight, at Mr Lewis' grave, nor could Mrs Johnson have known of his special interest in me nor of my affection for him. It had all happened when I was very young and I was not a child who discussed my inmost feelings with others, even my grandmother had no idea of the depth of affection the love-starved child I was had felt for Mr Lewis. I remembered the dead people I had seen in my childhood who had vanished so abruptly when I approached them and I felt these incidents tied up in some way with the things Mrs Johnson had said to me and to others in the hall. Yet I still doubted, I could not quite accept that the dead could, or would come back from wherever they might be, into the bare hall of the Friends' Meeting-house to relay messages to their friends through a lady as solid and earthly as Mrs Johnson. But the truth of what I had been told remained to nag at me and before I finally slept I made up my mind to investigate further.

And so for many weeks after that night I took my seat in the Friends' bare hall every Wednesday evening promptly at half past seven. At first I sat shyly in the rear as on the first occasion, but as I began to feel more at home and to become on friendly terms with one or two members of the congregation I ventured nearer and nearer to the front of the hall.

Gradually I came to appreciate the simplicity and sincerity of the short service of worship which on my first visit I had thought so naïve and unprofessional. I always tried to be sensible and objective about the clairvoyance which was given by various mediums after the service. I heard a great number of mediums at work during this period of my investigation into Spiritualism and by no means all of them impressed me favourably. In fact to only a very small number did I concede a genuine psychic gift, but at that stage I was not at all certain as to its nature. Was the medium really hearing or seeing the spirits of the dead or was it mind reading? Too many of the mediums seemed to me to fish for information from the people they singled out and then, having elaborated the information they got in this way, they handed it back as a message from the dead. At times I was sickened by the blatancy of this fishing and angered by the gullibility of the persons who accepted with enthusiasm evidence which I considered to be fraudulently obtained. Many times after hearing a medium of this kind I was tempted to give up the whole thing, but in those moments of disillusion I would remember the mediumship of Mrs Annie Johnson and soldier on.

I remember one medium who greatly impressed me. I have long since forgotten her name but I still have a mental picture of a dumpy little woman with improbable red hair wearing a poison-green chiffon dress with floating panels. During the service she as Mrs Johnson had done fell into trance but by this time I knew what was happening and I was not surprised when, still entranced, she walked to the edge of the platform and began to give an address. It did not even cause me to raise an eyebrow when the voice issuing from her lips turned out to be that of an educated and cultured man. I must admit, however, to a certain astonishment when she gave her clairvoyance in her waking state, for her own voice, undoubtedly that of a woman, was sheer gorblimey Cockney.

On rare occasions I received messages myself but I thought most of them could be explained easily enough by mind reading or prior knowledge. But on one or two occasions my young Arab turned up with the same message, I was to become a medium, I was to serve and help suffering humanity, to convince them that death was not the end, but for a long time I refused to accept it or even to think about it because it seemed to be utterly impossible, by no stretch of the imagination could I see myself standing on a platform giving messages in public.

These evenings at the Spiritualist meetings were not without their lighter moments. I began to recognise several people who attended regularly and who invariably stood up to claim messages which no one else present could accept or understand. 'Yes, yes...' they would exclaim eagerly, 'I know Jack' or Jim or William or whoever, 'he's my cousin in Spirit.' I used to think of them as the Body Snatchers and they afforded me a certain amount of quiet amusement. Years later I learned that all Spiritualist churches have these Old Faithfuls who grab at messages unclaimed by others but by then I had learned to be more sympathetic towards them since they are so often lonely or bereaved people longing to get some message of comfort and by snatching at obscure messages they hope that the medium will eventually give them something they can truly accept and understand.

One night after the officiating medium had described to me the young Arab 'who was not really an Arab' and given me the same message, that I must develop the mediumship I possessed, to serve my fellow man, which I was prepared to ignore as usual, I was approached after the meeting was over by a pleasant middle-aged woman who asked me what I was going to do about this message which she had heard given to me on more than one occasion. 'Nothing,' I mumbled, embarrassed, 'I'm not psychic, so what can I do about it?'

'You can come to my home circle and find out if these messages have any truth in them,' she said. 'If what you have been given is true then sitting in a circle will soon develop signs of mediumship if you have it.' I wanted to know what took place in this circle before I committed myself. The woman told me they sat round a very heavy Victorian dining-table and they were getting messages by rappings. I agreed to join them and after arranging an evening and a time I went home.

When I got home I found a letter propped up on the kitchen mantelpiece, addressed to me in handwriting I did not know and on the envelope a German stamp. I knew no one in Germany and, baffled, tore open the envelope. I was even more baffled when I read the letter inside. The letter, in eccentric English, was from a woman in Munich who said she had been sitting regularly for some years in a home circle and she had received a message through the medium of this circle from a spirit who called himself Rudolph Valentino. This spirit had given her my name and address in England and asked her to write to me and tell me he had tried to contact me through various mediums for a long time without much success. The message he wanted to give me was that I must develop my mediumship and be of service to my fellow men. I stood in our drab little kitchen for a long long time staring blankly into space. I read and re-read the mysterious letter and remembered the messages I had ignored. I wondered if 'the young Arab who was not really an Arab' could possibly be Valentino. I had seen and enjoyed two films of his in which he had played the part of an Arab, *The Sheik* and *The Son of the Sheik*, but did spirits really dress up in this way? Could it be an attempt to identify himself? If so, why should he suppose I would realise the mediums were describing him and not a real Arab? Even if it were Valentino, why should he want to contact me? I had never known him in life except as a shadow on the screen. True, I had admired him and I thought him very talented and enjoyed all his films but not more than many millions of others, so why pick on me? But argue as I might I could not get away from the fact that a woman in Germany of whom I had never heard and who I was equally certain had never heard of me had been given my correct name and address by a medium in Munich and had been asked to convey to me the same message which I had so often received, and ignored, from mediums in England. It was very late when I went to bed that night and the first light was in the sky before I slept.

Next day I wrote to the woman in Munich to tell her I had received her letter. I asked her if she would ask this spirit who called himself Rudolph Valentino if he would make himself known to me in England in some way which would be convincing to me.

The night of the home circle came and I arrived at the house early as my hostess had suggested in order to get to know the other members of the circle before we started the proceedings. When we were all present we were six, three women and three men. The seance was to be held in a room in which was the large Victorian dining-table which my hostess had described. That night she told me the table could also be used as a billiard-table and her husband and son often used it for this purpose. We seated ourselves round the table and my hostess turned down the gaslight, leaving just enough light for us to see each other quite clearly, and we all placed our hands palms down on the surface of the table.

When we had been sitting like this for ten minutes or so a loud rap was heard apparently from the centre of the table. My hostess said this meant the spirits were ready to communicate with us. She went on to explain that they had worked out with the spirits a means of communication which, though it was slow and laborious, worked very well. One member of the circle would go slowly through the alphabet and at the required letter there would be a rap. Another member of the circle was charged with writing down the letters and later reading out the message. First the spirits welcomed me as a newcomer to the circle, then they conveyed the message that I had great power. This was meant in the psychic sense, of course. The next message informed us that I had brought a spirit with me who wanted to give me a message, and they said this spirit with me had been very psychically gifted in his lifetime, they said his name was Valentino. The next message, supposedly from Valentino, was exactly the same message contained in the letter from Munich and I was asked to thank the German lady for delivering it.

We were then asked if we would like to see how much greater the power was because of my presence. When we all said we would, the heavy table gave a great lurch, then reared itself up to stand on one end. When I considered the weight and size of this table I could hardly believe the evidence of my eyes. After this happening the messages continued and we were told we could in future dispense with the table and just sit quietly in a circle. They would experiment with the power, we were told, and particularly with me because I had remarkable physical mediumship, in fact they hoped later on to be able to speak to us in direct voice.

After the seance coffee and cakes were provided and we discussed the evening's events while we ate and drank companionably. All the members of the circle were delighted with the results and told me they had never had so startling a manifestation before. They asked me to continue sitting with their circle and I promised to do so, then took my leave of them.

I walked home through the darkened town with much food for thought. To what had I committed myself by agreeing to continue with this circle, did I really want to be a medium at all? All the way home I pondered the night's events and finally I came to the conclusion that it was true. The dead could communicate.

Three

FOR a day or two after the seance at the house of the lady I
now knew as Mrs Cook I was elated by my new-found conviction, but as the day of the next session approached my doubts
about becoming a medium grew. Somehow I could not
imagine myself standing on a platform in front of a congregation, describing spirits and relaying messages. I felt I was too
young and no one would take me seriously, particularly as I
had noticed that church congregations, both orthodox and
Spiritualist, seemed to consist largely of older people. It was
the exception rather than the rule to see someone of my age
among them. There was also the fact that I had always desperately wanted to do something of an artistic nature as my life's
work, although I knew it would be hard to realise this ambition since I had no education to speak of, and I knew no one
who might help me to get out of the rut poverty and circum-
stance had created for me. None the less I had hopes of finding a better paid job one day and then I would be able to pay
for lessons and study art.

My decision wavered this way and that and the day I was
due at Mrs Cook's house got nearer and nearer. I knew if I
went on the appointed day I would morally be committed to
attend every week for an indefinite period, weeks, months,
even years for all I knew. After much deep thought I finally
decided to be content with the conviction I had been given
that there was life after death and forget those grandiose no-

tions of serving humanity in order to get on with my own life. I would not return to Mrs Cook's house. I wrote a polite note to her telling her of my decision, but before I could post it another letter arrived from Munich. In it my unknown correspondent told me Valentino had spoken again through the medium of her circle and had instructed her to write and plead with me to carry out his request to develop my mediumship and to tell me he would help me and he and I together would help humanity to find the truth. He had said he wanted to repay a little of the affection ordinary men and women had shown him in his lifetime and by helping my development as a medium he felt he would do so. This letter had arrived by the first post before I left for my day's work, and on the kitchen mantelpiece where I had left it the previous night to remind me to post it on my way to the cemetery was my letter to Mrs Cook. I looked at the German letter and I looked at the envelope on the mantelpiece. What should I do? In the end I put both letters in my pocket. I would think things over during the day and if I decided to ignore the letter from Munich I could post my note to Mrs Cook on my way home from work that night.

That day there was a funeral which I found even more harrowing than usual. The chief mourner, a middle-aged woman in the sombre weeds widows wore in those days, was distraught with grief and while the elderly parson gabbled through the burial service her friends had to restrain her from throwing herself into the open grave. When the service was over and the widow's friends were leading her away she caught hold of the parson's arm and I heard her say to him in a voice choked with tears, 'How can I leave him all alone in that horrible hole? I can't go on without him, I can't!' The clergyman spoke kindly to her. 'It was God's will to take Jim before you, ask Him for the grace to resign yourself to Him and He will comfort you.' The widow gave a kind of strangled scream, 'If it's God's will to take him and leave me all alone, I hate Him, I hate Him!' 'Please, Mrs Wilson, control yourself!' said the parson sharply. He turned to the friends holding the woman's arms, 'Get her home as quickly as possible!' The friends persuaded the widow in the direction of the waiting cars and the parson walked briskly off in the opposite direction. Impulsively I started towards the grief-stricken woman, I wanted to tell her she had not lost her husband for ever, he was still near her, loving and caring for her as always, but I checked myself abruptly and stood stockstill in the middle of the gravel path. What right had I to intrude on this woman's grief? She would see my mud-caked dungarees and think I was impertinent and presumptuous, and how could I comfort her even if she listened to me? Only a medium could do that, a human bridge between the living and the dead. I stood for some moments with this thought hammering in my mind, then slowly I drew the envelope addressed to Mrs Cook from my pocket, I looked at it, hesitating, then I tore it across and across and dropped the pieces in a refuse bin. Now I had committed myself. I would try to develop as a medium if that was what was required of me.

On the night of the circle Mrs Cook and her friends gave me a big welcome, and their warmth and kindness made up for a feeling I had that somehow I had given up my freedom. One of the men in Mrs Cook's circle who had been introduced the previous week as Mr Herbert was late, and when he finally came it seemed to me he brought with him a great wave of sadness, but no one else seemed to notice anything untoward and Mrs Cook suggested we form our chairs into a circle and dispense with the table in obedience to the instructions we had been given last time we sat. The gas was turned down low and we began the seance by singing a hymn. Mrs Cook then said a simple prayer asking for protection and offering the circle for God's purpose, and we sat in silence waiting for a sign. I wondered what would happen and regretted the loss of the table which had been used before for such an interesting manifestation. The clock on the chimney-piece ticked loudly and the homely sound soothed and reassured me. We waited a long time, nothing happened and the heat of the room made me feel drowsy, but at the same time I had a feeling of great well-being, finally I remembered nothing more for I fell fast asleep.

When I awoke the rest of the circle were still in their places just as they were when I fell asleep. I wondered what on earth they must think of me and started to apologise but Mrs Cook cut me short by saying a prayer which was clearly meant to close the proceedings and I shut up. The gas was turned up and Mrs Cook went out to fetch refreshments. One of the women turned to me with a beaming smile. 'It was a wonderful sitting,' she said. I felt worse than ever, not only had I been rude to these kind people but I had missed the wonders as well. 'I'm sorry,' I mumbled awkwardly, 'the room was so warm I couldn't keep awake.' Mr Herbert smiled at me kindly. 'You were not asleep, you were in trance,' he said. 'You are a natural born medium.' I stared at him in utter disbelief. 'My wife talked to me,' went on Mr Herbert. I was glad he was pleased and looked so much happier than when he arrived but I still found it hard to believe. Mrs Cook returned with a trolley laden with refreshments and she, too, was beaming approval at me.

As we drank tea and ate egg-and-cress sandwiches which were a thought too dainty for my appetite I heard more snippets of what had been going on while I was asleep or in trance or whatever I had been. The other woman's sweetheart, who had been killed in the war, had talked to her, and the other man had had a talk with his mother. All very well for them, I was thinking rather sourly, they've had a whale of an evening but it's been a total blank for me. I hoped they would go back to the table next time and let me be part of the proceedings. Mrs Cook offered me a plate of iced cakes. 'I nearly forgot,' she said casually, 'a film actor came through, Valentine or whatever he called himself, the one that died a couple of years ago.' 'Valentino?' I ventured. 'That's the one,' said Mrs Cook, 'he said to tell you to continue with your development.' 'Of course he can't be a very advanced soul and as you develop in our circle we shall hope to contact entities a lot more spiritually evolved than Hollywood actors.' What a cheek, I thought, who is she to say who is advanced and who isn't? How was I to know at this stage of our acquaintance that Mrs Cook claimed to be guided by a very exalted spirit known as Shu-Shu who had been a high priestess in the temple of Isis during her life on earth, and for this reason Mrs Cook was determined to keep her circle on the very highest level, both spiritually and intellectually. Unfortunately, no one warned me about Shu-Shu who was eventually to be the means of my fall from grace in the Cook circle.

That night I walked part of the way home with Mr Herbert, hoping he would tell me more about what Valentino had said while I was blanked out. I was out of luck, he talked without ceasing about his wife who, it seemed, had died with tragic suddenness some months before. Their marriage had been ideal, he said, and without her life had been bleak and lonely until she had spoken to him through me during the seance that evening. Naturally I was glad I had been the means of giving back meaning to his life but I did wish he would spare the time to answer my timid questions about Valentino and his message for me. I wanted to know what his voice had sounded like, was it an American voice or an Italian-accented one, and above all was any evidence given that it really was Valentino? Since Mrs Cook had not even said his name correctly I could not be sure about this. But Mr Herbert was too wrapped up in his own experience to bother to answer me explicitly. I gave up trying and we walked on in silence, until quite suddenly he shot a question at me. 'You were talking to the others for some time before I arrived, were you not?' he asked. I told him I had arrived punctually and had chatted with the others until he came. 'I suppose they told you about my wife's tragic death?' he said quite sharply. 'No,' I replied, 'as a matter of fact no one even mentioned you or your wife.' 'I shall check up on that,' he said, 'so I hope you are telling the truth.' Somewhat huffily I said I wasn't in the habit of telling lies. Mr Herbert stopped short in a pool of light under a lamp-post and turned me by the shoulders to face him. He looked very solemn. He said the communication from his wife meant far too much to him to accept it at face value. He wanted to be certain it was not just a production of my subconscious or even my conscious mind. If I developed as a medium I must expect to be doubted at times and only charlatans and fakes resented being investigated by intelligent people. I said I saw that, but what I saw even more clearly was that being a medium was going to be tough if everyone suspected you were a liar or a fake all the time. Mr Herbert was not done with me. 'Another thing, Flint,' he went on. 'It's a big thing for an ordinary working lad to sit in a circle like Mrs Cook's, so live cleanly and be worthy of the chance.' Even if we haven't a bathroom in our house I bet I'm as clean as you are, I thought, but I just said I must hurry home in case my grandmother worried, and he let me go.

I sat regularly in Mrs Cook's circle for many months and the procedure hardly varied from the first time. Since Mrs Cook wanted her circle to be highly spiritual we always began with a hymn and prayers, then I would 'go off' as they put it and various spirits would speak through me. At least the others told me afterwards that they did, but as far as I was concerned it was just a lost hour in my life, I saw nothing and heard nothing, and I had to rely on what snippets of information I could pick up from others when I came out of trance. However, I liked the hymns and the prayers, and the sandwiches and cakes at the end of the seance were delicious. Also the others kept telling me how well I was developing so I was encouraged to persevere.

One night after I had been sitting in this circle for over a year Mrs Cook herself fell into trance and the spirit called Shu-Shu spoke to us. Shu-Shu urged us not to encourage entities near to the earth plane as we had been doing but to aspire to communicate with more advanced and progressed souls.

From that night on my trances gradually became less and less until they stopped altogether, and Mrs Cook and Shu-Shu took over. I wondered if my development had stopped. I was puzzled and so were the other members of the circle with the exception of Mrs Cook who was convinced her guide Shu-Shu had arranged matters in this way so that the circle would become more spiritual and not be content merely to communicate with their friends and relations on the other side through my mediumship. To do justice to Mrs Cook, she was deeply concerned that I should develop what she said was great potential in the most elevated conditions possible. To that end, as circle leader she ordained we sing more hymns and say more prayers in future.

I continued to sit in the circle regularly but now I could hear all that went on which, since Mrs Cook had developed her trance mediumship, was usually Shu-Shu giving an elevated discourse full of words whose meaning I did not know but which I thought must be very educated.

One night when Mrs Cook was in trance, Shu-Shu said she would demonstrate through her medium one of the rituals she used to perform when she was a high priestess in the temple of Isis. We all said it would be a privilege to see this and begged her to do us this honour. Mrs Cook was far from being a sylph, she was broad in the beam and her bosoms were of Earth Mother proportions. In trance, this substantial figure rose from her chair and moved to the centre of the circle where she began to dance. She gyrated her hips and weaved her arms, the while chanting what sounded gibberish to me but was acclaimed enthusiastically by the others as ancient Egyptian. The bounteous bosoms flopped alarmingly as the dance grew more energetic, first to one side then to the other, and the arms kept weaving like the tentacles of a busy octopus. I wanted to look away, I was embarrassed for Mrs Cook, but try as I might my eyes were glued to the spectacle. I knew it would happen, I tried desperately to stop it but I started to giggle, at first subdued by sheer will power to a series of

43

choked hiccoughs, but as the gyrating and the weaving and the flopping went on I completely lost control of myself and I laughed and laughed until the tears streamed down my face. The more shocked and angry the other members of the circle looked, the more I laughed until at last Mrs Cook came out of her trance and with a look which withered me to ashes sat down in her chair again.

Later, when Mrs Cook saw me to the front door to bid me good night it was no surprise to me when she said, quite kindly, under the circumstances, 'I really think, dear, you are still too young and perhaps too excitable to continue your development at present. It would be best if you didn't come here again.' She opened the door and I saw it was raining heavily outside. On a wage of 12s 6d a week a raincoat was not a luxury I could afford so I prepared to sally forth and be drenched. But kind, forgiving Mrs Cook, to soften the blow she had dealt me, put her arms round me with the obvious intention of giving me an affectionate farewell kiss. I was touched by her generosity but, reluctant to be pressed to that bounteous bosom, I stepped aside and with all the gaucherie of my seventeen years trod heavily on her foot. 'Right on my corn, you clumsy oaf!' she cried in agony, and mumbling apologies I went out into the night and the rain.

Squelching home in my leaking shoes I thought over the night's humiliating events. I grew more and more depressed and ashamed of myself. I had been given a rare opportunity to develop my mediumship in a circle of educated, spiritual and posh people and I had ruined my chances and insulted the leader of the circle. Added to this, the exalted Shu-Shu had said I worked on a low vibration so what use could I ever be to help and uplift humanity as Valentino had promised I would do? Now the circle did not want me, no one wanted me, I had failed miserably and I would never be a medium of any value to the world. By the time I had reached home and was sitting in the kitchen drinking the cocoa my grandmother made for

me I had made my decision. I would give up the whole business of trying to be a medium, I would have nothing more to do
with Spiritualism, instead I would get on with my own life
and try to make something worth while of it.

Four

PALE eyes bored into mine and the bony finger flailed the air an inch from my nose. 'Do you think a steady job like this grows on the hedges? You are going to rue this day, my lad, I'm telling you.' My guts lurched at the very thought of being out of work but I had made up my mind to escape from the dead and I stuck to my guns. 'I'll work out my notice but I want to leave the cemetery.' I finally got out through dry lips. 'Don't you imagine you can crawl back here when you've worn out your shoe leather looking for work.' I dodged the finger. 'Once you walk out of these gates I wash my hands of you.' Mr Hobbs stalked off, tut-tutting at the rashness and folly of the younger generation. I tried to cheer myself with the thought that I might find a job before my next and last pay-day at the cemetery, but those guts of mine lurched again at a mental picture of the long queue at the local 'Labour'. I had burnt my boats, I had crossed my Rubicon, in one week's time I would be a member of that hopeless queue.

During my last week at the cemetery my grandmother listened avidly to the talk about jobs in the local post office but she heard of nothing for me, and on Friday I was paid off for the last time with the terrifying prospect of being 'out' for heaven only knew how long.

I read the Situations Vacant column in the local paper each time it came out and one day I saw 'Willing Lad for duties as pageboy. Apply in person to the Manager Regent Cinema St

46

Albans,' I was willing enough, so I shot off like a bullet from a gun to apply for the job, and simply because the uniform worn by the previous pageboy fitted me like a glove I was lucky enough to be taken on, disappointing the many other willing lads who had applied. What joy it was to be in work again, the scared ashamed feeling of being 'out' left me almost immediately, and I told myself that no lad would ever be as willing as I would be. I might even learn about film projection if I kept my eyes and ears open, I could rise one day to be the manager of a cinema myself, a vista of golden opportunity opened out before me, and the pay was my accustomed 12s 6d a week, so my rash folly had paid off.

My duties at the cinema, which was the same my grandmother and I had patronised began at nine o'clock in the morning when I appeared punctually in working clothes to sweep out the cinema, scrub the vestibule and make myself generally useful until three p.m. when I had two hours off. At five o'clock, wearing my inherited uniform, I was standing at the cinema entrance to keep the various queues in order. I tried to stop them causing an obstruction on the pavement, I pounced on those who sneaked ahead of others who had waited longer and coaxed them back into line, I answered politely such questions as 'Has the film got a happy ending?' or 'Is there a Gents' handy in the fourpennies?' My day ended when the cinema closed at ten-thirty. It was a long day but I did not mind because in addition to my 12s 6d wage I had the delightful perquisite of moments when I could watch the film from the door at the back of the stalls. These snatches of watching could add up to nearly the whole film in three days and as the programme changed mid-weekly, I could see almost two films in a week, more than I could ever afford in the days when I had to pay for a tip-up seat.

There was a dance-hall in the lower part of the cinema building where a dance was held every Saturday night. I had to be on duty in the gentlemen's cloakroom on these occasions to hand out numbered tickets in exchange for hats and coats,

47

and when things were quiet in the cloakroom I would carry round trays of drinks at the barman's behest. I was not paid extra for these dance nights, but I was given a saucer to put on the cloakroom counter into which the customers would drop a penny or twopence when they handed in or collected their garments and these tips were my perquisite. On occasion the coppers in the saucer might add up to a cool 3s and I considered myself amply recompensed.

I began to take an interest in the dancing on these Saturday nights. Whenever I was free for a few minutes I would stand at the edge of the dance floor watching the dancers, envying their expertise. In those days they were dancing the foxtrot, the waltz, the tango and, a new craze, the Charleston. I longed to be able to do the dances I saw and I would watch the dancers, memorising the steps, then dash into my cloakroom to try them out before I forgot them. Eventually I thought I might make a fair showing at most of the ballroom dances, and I longed to be able to practise with a partner. This was impossible, it was as much as my job was worth to approach any of the lady patrons of the dance-hall, so I contented myself with the mop which was kept in the cloakroom, holding it in my arms and imagining it was one of the attractive girls I had seen on the dance floor, and even if my imagination had to work overtime the mop was better than no one at all.

One night the mop and I were practising the waltz when we were interrupted by one of the patrons whose dancing I had often admired from my vantage point at the edge of the dance floor. From the expression on his face when he saw me dancing so earnestly with the mop, he thought I had gone out of my mind, so when he asked me what on earth I was doing, though I felt a perfect ninny, I told him. To my astonishment he removed the mop and took me in his arms, 'Let me show you a new step which hasn't even reached St Albans yet,' he offered, and started to waltz me round the cloakroom illustrating the new step as we went. But I was learning the wrong way round because I had to follow his lead as if I were the

48

lady. I was trying to get the hang of the new step well enough to be able to practise it the right way round with the mop later when the lesson ended abruptly with the entrance of the manager. The manager looked very black, he asked my teacher to return to the dance floor or to leave if he preferred it. The patron seemed confused and embarrassed and hurried out, which left me to face the wrath of the manager alone. I expected the worst, we were not supposed to be familiar with the paying guests, but the manager spoke quite kindly. 'Keep away from that man,' he said, 'he's queer.' I had never heard the word in a homosexual context so I suppose I looked baffled. 'Well, never mind, attend to your duties properly in future, and if I find you with him again, you'll be sacked on the spot.' He went out, leaving me to wonder if my would-be teacher had escaped from Shenley Asylum or something, but I was determined to avoid him like the plague from then onwards in case I lost my job.

As the weeks passed and I went on practising with the mop I began to long more and more for a real girl as a partner, and finally I decided that my Saturday coppers would pay for dancing lessons on my one free night a week. I scouted round and enrolled in Miss Florence's School of Dancing where I would be given lessons in modern ballroom dancing on my free evening for 2s a session.

Miss Florence's School was held in a large bare room at the back of an office building. Music for the lessons was provided sometimes by an elderly lady pianist, at others by a cabinet gramophone which I preferred because I thought it was more like the music at a real dance.

Miss Florence was an excellent teacher and after a few months of her tuition I was proficient enough to decide to stop my lessons and devote my night off and my 2s to escorting a fair-haired girl I had my eye on to real dances. With this in mind I arrived at the school for the lesson I intended to be my last and when it was over I lingered after the rest of the class had gone to tell Miss Florence I was not coming back again.

49

To my surprise she offered to continue my lessons free of charge if I would give her some help with her more backward pupils. Naturally I was flattered but I wanted to have fun on future nights off and I refused as politely as I could.

Miss Florence was tall, slim, elegant and self-assured and I could hardly believe my ears when she actually pleaded with me to stay on in the class. The reason emerged as we talked and I found myself pitying this aloof, poised lady who had seemed so far removed from the squalid little problems which fretted ordinary people like me. It turned out Miss Florence had to support an elderly ailing mother and the school was not making enough money to employ a second teacher to give individual attention to the slower pupils and consequently they were threatening to take their custom elsewhere. Whether my vanity or my sympathy was titillated the more by Miss Florence's confidence I do not know to this day but, banishing the pleasing picture of myself and my blonde heart-throb gliding together over some ballroom floor to the spontaneous applause of the onlookers, I agreed to remain in the class on Miss Florence's terms.

I was soon to discover the backward pupils were either men or overweight and rigidly corseted matrons, and trying to instil in them the joys of the dance was heavy going indeed. How I longed to go to a real dance with a real partner who would follow my lead and feel light as a feather in my arms but unless I changed my job for one which left me free in the evenings it seemed unlikely I would ever get the chance. I remembered the shamed feeling of being out of work too vividly to risk giving up the job I had in the hope of finding another. I tried to console myself with the thought that at least I was keeping up with all the newest steps.

One Saturday night at work when the cinema programme was almost over, one of the usherettes asked me to turn on the main switch which controlled the lights in the dance-hall. I rushed off like the eager beaver I was to do her bidding. The main switchboard was housed in a small room off the vestibule and in I went. I surveyed the big board about which I knew less than nothing. I saw two levers which looked to me like main switches but I had no idea which one of them controlled the dance-hall lights so, to make sure, I pulled them both. There was a bang, a flash, smoke billowed from the switchboard and the light went out. Guiltily I crept out into the vestibule to find total darkness and chaos. Patrons were running around shouting, the manager, waving a torch, frantically promised to refund money later, usherettes waved torches to show panic-stricken people the way out, women cried, children howled, strong men pushed and shoved their way to the exits. In that Stygian darkness one thing was as clear as day, there would be no more business done in either cinema or dance-hall that night. There was the inevitable post mortem on the following Monday and I learned I had blown the main fuse of the entire building and through my stupidity the company had lost hundreds of pounds. The sentence of the manager at this drumhead court martial was instant dismissal. I became a member of the dispirited queue at the local Labour Exchange and for the first time in my working life I was on the dole.

Week followed hopeless week and the scared, shamed feeling of the workless was with me all the time. I walked miles looking for work and when the soles of my one decent pair of shoes were worn through my grandmother cut out new soles from thick cardboard and when she had polished the uppers with Cherry Blossom and elbow grease I was respectable again.

Eventually the clerk at the 'Labour' asked me if I would leave my home town and take a job as a barman in a London public house. This offer put me in a quandary. My grandmother depended on the few shillings I squeezed from my dole money to help her to exist and if I left St Albans I wondered how she would manage to live. I was wondering how to solve this dilemma when I saw the contemptuous look on the clerk's face, it said as clearly as if he had spoken how much he despised the workshy lower class who were always moaning about jobs and houses but when they were offered work refused it and when they were rehoused kept coal in the bath. I would solve Gran's problem later as best I could, I accepted the job in London.

As it turned out, the public house was not actually in the heart of London as I had imagined, it was in Barkingside, Essex, then a fairly country district with grass and trees instead of the grimy streets and frowning buildings I had dreaded. The pub where I was to work was the Fairlop Oak and it was managed by a warm-hearted Irish couple who greeted me when I arrived like a long lost friend instead of the new pot-boy and general factotum. I was shown into a clean little bedroom and told it was to be my very own and this was an especial joy because as long as I could remember I had had to share the upstairs bedroom in my grandmother's house with the lodger who kept me awake with his whistling gurgling snores. Not only was I to have the privacy of my own room but its window overlooked the garden and I woke up to the sight of trees and the sound of birds.

Mr and Mrs Ryan were patient with my mistakes and encouraged my efforts to learn the trade and for this very reason I picked up the work quickly. Before long I had graduated from pot-boy and fire lighter to more responsible duties in the cellar and then to serving behind the bar. I enjoyed the bar work and I grew quite fond of some of the regular customers who had their own tankards with their names on them displayed on a special shelf. The 'Oak' was a cheerful and well-run house and I was happy there. I remember Mr Ryan's passion for the records of John McCormack, the Irish tenor, and how all day long we worked to the sound of the golden voice singing all the Irish ballads the Ryans loved. Whenever I hear 'Danny Boy', 'Killarney', 'Mother Machree' or any of the others even now I am transported back to the 'Oak' and I wish the Ryans well wherever they may be.

On my days off I used to take the bus into Town and spend my time visiting the museums and art galleries, occasionally going to the pictures. I began to think again of cutting a swathe in some dance-hall, but when I compared my one and only suit with the suits of the men I saw Up West I realised I was too shabby to venture into any of them. Obviously I must buy a suit, but however long I window-shopped I found nothing cheaper than 30s, which was an astronomical sum for anyone earning my wage. It looked as if I was foiled again, but kind Mr Ryan came to my rescue and advanced me the 30s for my suit if I undertook to repay the loan at 5s a week. This meant I had to postpone my terpsichorean triumphs until my debt was paid so that I could continue to send my grandmother a small postal order each week. At last the great occasion came and, wearing my new suit, shoes shining, hair slicked flat and with ten reckless shillings in my pocket I caught a bus and rode all the way to Piccadilly Circus in breathless excitement.

I had already decided to patronise the Astoria Dance Hall in Charing Cross Road because I had been told ladies were to be found there who would dance without the formality of an introduction. When I arrived I was dumb with wonder, the mirror surface of the floor, the big band in smart uniforms, the exotic décor and the coloured lights playing over the dancers were to me the summit of elegance and chic. I felt I was mingling on equal terms with the gilded youth of London. For a few minutes I stood on the sidelines to observe procedure. As far as I could judge one simply chose one of the bevy of unaccompanied beauties, walked up to her and asked her to dance. Feeling very daring I approached a dazzling blonde. She slid into my arms and soon we were circling the floor in fine style, exchanging brilliant snippets of small talk like did she come there often and what did I think of the band. I am bound to admit none of the other dancers broke into spontaneous applause for our performance but I felt I was not letting Miss Florence down.

I danced with various partners, but I kept on returning to my blonde dazzler not only because she was a good dancer but she had a trick of welding her body to mine which I found very exciting. In those days familiarity between the sexes was by no means as immediate as it is today and I was very thrilled when she said I could call her Muriel.

At the end of the evening I had a problem. I wanted to dance the last waltz with Muriel but this would imply that I would take her home and I had no idea where she lived. I would gladly walk with her to Land's End but a beautiful girl such as she was would undoubtedly expect a taxi and what with my entrance fee and the lemonades I had bought for my partners I had half-a-crown left for my bus fare home and to see me through until next pay day. There was only one answer, I would not dance the last waltz at all, if I could not dance with Muriel I was not going to slight her by taking another partner. I was standing rather gloomily on the sidelines watching the last dance when two soft hands were clapped over my eyes, and I turned to find her smiling at me. 'Will you walk home with me?' she asked. 'My flat is only a few steps from here.' I was caught up at once into the seventh heaven of bliss.

The soft light from the street lamps made a nimbus of the blonde hair and Muriel looked very lovely to me as we walked down a narrow dingy street and stopped outside a door with paint peeling in strips between a barber's shop and a wine store with its windows still lit up. Muriel opened the peeling door with her key to reveal a steep flight of wooden stairs. 'Follow me,' she said brightly. I muttered something about catching my bus. 'Oh, come up for a short time,' she insisted and taking my hand she pulled me up the stairs with her.

I looked round Muriel's room vaguely wondering what was wrong with it. The furniture was shabby, but I was used to shabbiness, it was something else. It was a pink, frilly feminine room, there was a big Kewpie doll in a feathered headdress on the mantelpiece and a pink teddy-bear lay on the bedcover. A chintz curtain, riotous with sunflowers, concealed a gas stove and a shelf with pots and pans. Suddenly I knew what was wrong, I missed the soap and wax polish smell which pervaded my grandmother's home. This room was neglected, not quite clean. Muriel opened a wardrobe and took out a black filmy garment which she slung casually round her neck, and after excusing herself she left the room. Shortly I heard a tap running and wondered hopefully if she was filling a kettle for tea.

Shortly the tap was turned off and Muriel came back into the room, wearing the black filmy thing, and underneath it she was stark naked. I had had no experience to guide me in a situation of this kind so I suppose I just stood, rooted to the spot, looking the country bumpkin which in truth I was. Briskly my blonde divinity pulled back the bedcover and turned down the sheets. 'Don't be scared if it's your first time, Muriel will show you the ropes.' Five minutes later, crushed, crumpled and ashamed, I was standing in the middle of the floor again. I stammered something about the bus and really having to go and made for the door, before I got there Muriel was facing me like an avenging angel. 'You'll put my five bob on the mantelpiece before you set foot outside that door,' she shrilled. I stared at her in utter disbelief. In my naïvety I thought the two of us had been carried away by a sudden irresistible urge and though I was ashamed of giving way to what I thought of as my lust it had not entered my mind the transaction could be financial.

When Muriel cottoned on to the fact I simply could not pay the 5s she told me exactly what she thought of me and she did not mince her words or spare my feelings. By the time she had done with me I felt as if I had been through a mangle and when disdainfully she ordered me to get out of her sight, thankfully I went. As I crept stealthily down the wooden stairs she appeared at the top to hurl a last insult, 'You and your thirty bob suit!' she spat venomously and vanished from view.

All the way back to Barkingside in between bouts of guilt and shame I kept wondering how Muriel could have known how much I paid for my suit, but when I reached the sanctuary of my little room at the Fairlop Oak I saw the price tag was still hanging from the tab at the back of the jacket collar.

I had heard a great deal about the new talking picture at the Regal Cinema, Marble Arch; it was *The Singing Fool* starring Al Jolson, and all my customers in the bar raved about it. The more I thought about a picture talking and in this case even singing, the more wonderful it seemed and the more I longed to see and hear it.

At last the day came when I took my place in the long queue which stretched far down the Edgware Road prepared to inch forward with the rest for as long as it took to get into the Regal to see this new wonder, and after standing for two hours or more I sat down in my tip-up seat feeling all the usual thrill of anticipation and more as the lights were lowered.

The film had not run for longer than a very few minutes before I knew its canned music could never replace the orchestral accompaniment to the big silent films. The actors' voices sounded strange and harsh, reminding me of very early gramophone records and the magic the silent films had for me was simply not there. The people on the screen were no longer beautiful, glamorous or mysterious, their voices were tinny and did not match the way they looked. This new miracle struck me as artificial and deadly dull. I came out of the Regal convinced the new craze for talking pictures could not last.

It was a long time before I went to a talking picture again, instead I would seek out the small cinemas which had not been able to afford to instal the expensive sound equipment and revel in the old silent films they were forced to show. I remember one manager of such a cinema who put a placard outside his doors announcing 'Silence is Golden' and I agreed with him all the way.

In the early days of the talkies, which to my surprise continued to thrive, many of Hollywood's greatest stars disappeared from the film galaxy because their voices were unsuitable or discordant and I began to think of Rudolph Valentino again. I wondered if his voice would have matched his grace and good looks or whether he too would have been destroyed by sound. I thought perhaps he was fortunate to have died when he did before the legend he had created could be ridiculed out of existence. Thinking in this way, I remembered those messages from Germany which begged me to develop mediumship, to serve the world. I wondered what Valentino thought of me now if truly the messages had come from him. I was certainly serving spirits but hardly the kind he meant me to serve, but I had made my decision to get on with my life in my own way so I pushed these thoughts to the back of my mind and forgot about Valentino.

Some time later on my day off I decided to go to a live theatre. After shopping around I decided to patronise the Prince of Wales' Theatre where they were performing what I took to be a nautical play called *Outward Bound*. I had always enjoyed films about the sea and I had read *Moby Dick* so I set off for the theatre expecting to be well entertained. *Outward Bound* had very little to do with the sea but it had a great deal to do with life after death. True, I enjoyed the play, I thought it was a great and moving experience, but it seemed to me the dead had caught up with me again, I was not to be allowed to escape what I had been told was my duty to mankind, stupid as it may sound now I felt my choice of this particular play had been forced upon me as a sort of ghostly nudge towards the path I was expected to tread.

'That night in my little room at the Fairlop Oak I lay awake for hours thinking about the play, wondering if I should give up my job and go home to St Albans to try and find a new group of people who would sit with me and help me to develop my mediumship. Common sense warned me I could not lightly give up a job I liked and where I was happy without any real excuse, and if I did I would get no dole money from the Labour Exchange while I was out of work. I tossed and turned in my narrow bed wondering what to do, arguing with myself, first this way, then that, until at last I fell asleep.

I awoke next morning bug-eyed, but knowing exactly what I was going to do. Then and there I gave Mr Ryan the customary two weeks' notice and when my next day off came round I bought a cheap day return ticket and took the train to St Albans.

It was pleasant to be in my own home town again but I had a flock of butterflies fluttering in my stomach whenever I thought how rash I had been giving up my good job at the Fairlop Oak without any immediate prospect of another. As I wandered up the main street on my way to my grandmother's house I saw a card in the window of a tailor's shop. 'Young Man Wanted' it said. How I hoped I was the young man they wanted, I certainly wanted them. I went into the shop and asked to see the manager. He came out of the back premises and I asked if I might be considered for the vacancy. I answered his every question to the best of my ability, even telling him about my disaster in the cinema which, to my relief, made him laugh. Eventually the butterflies swirling and fluttering in my stomach folded their wings and slept when he accepted me for the job. The wage was my standard rate of 12s 6d a week and my duties were to include keeping the shop clean, polishing the show windows, delivering orders and any other tasks at which I could make myself useful. The last hurdle was crossed when he agreed to keep the job open for me while I worked out my notice in London. Once more I had burnt my boats and crossed my Rubicon, I wondered what I would find on the other side.

Five

I LIKED my job at John Maxwell's Ready-to-Wear shop for men, the duties were lighter than any I had previously known. the manager and his assistant were kindly and I had my evenings to myself. In the morning I swept out, dusted and polished the shop then standing on a step ladder on the pavement I washed and polished the big show windows until they shone. At least they shone to within a foot of the top because I have never had any head for heights and it was only on rare occasions I could force myself on to the top step of the ladder to do the job thoroughly. For the rest of the day I did any odd job required of me, ran errands and delivered purchases to customers' homes.

At my grandmother's home where I was again living I sadly missed the privacy of my own room which had been such a joy to me at the Fairlop Oak. I had to share a bedroom with George, the elderly lodger, once more and try to ignore his snoring and his morning smell of stale sweat and last night's beer. At this time George was in his early sixties, a taciturn man with the ruddy complexion of the countryman and a long mournfully drooping moustache. Some time in the 1870s he had started work as a stable lad at The Old Mile House, an old coaching inn one mile from St Albans, and he still worked there. For many years George had groomed the horses and polished the carriages of the gentry until the triumph of the motor-car had closed the stables and reduced George to handyman at a wage of one pound a week. Like my grand-mother he could neither read nor write and he never stopped grumbling about the disappearance of his beloved horses from the roads or failed to curse the noise and stink of the 'moty-cars'.

We had a parlour in our house which was always known as the front room. It was furnished with stiff Victorian armchairs, a round mahogany table covered with a cloth edged with bobbles and sundry what-nots filled with bric-à-brac. There was a sideboard on which stood a tantalus containing two glass decanters which never to my knowledge had held liquor and which in my childhood had vanished into the pawnshop during periods of greater financial crisis than usual. There were two sets of curtains at the window, lace ones which were washed every Monday and heavy velvet drapes which were kept half-drawn during the day in case the sun faded the patterned rug which lay rakishly askew on the worn linoleum. There was red crinkled paper pleated into a fan in the empty grate and the pottery vase holding dried bulrushes which stood in one corner could be thought to provide that touch which traditionally only a woman's hand can give. It was an important part of my grandmother's image of respectability to have a parlour and she took great pride in her own. The mahogany furniture was polished until it shone and she would get down on her knees to scrub the linoleum, and when it was dry she would get on her knees again to polish it with Ronuk floor polish. Each worthless piece of bric-à-brac from the laden what-nots was washed in hot soapy water and dried with loving care once a week. She spent hours mending the holes worn in her lace curtains by age and too frequent washing, darning them with small exquisite stitches, trying to recreate the pattern which had gone.

It would have been quite unthinkable to use this Holy of Holies on any lesser occasion than Christmas Day or the funeral of a close relative and so we sat in the kitchen at all other times.

When George and I came in from our work we were given a meal which was called tea but in reality it was our main meal of the day. We would have pie and peas, sausages and mashed potatoes or scrag-end of mutton stew, washed down with mugs of strong tea and accompanied by unlimited bread and margarine. When tea was over the three of us would draw close to the minuscule fire in the kitchen grate, Gran in her wicker armchair mending or knitting, George with his feet up on the sagging horsehair sofa smoking his clay pipe and I sitting bolt upright on a kitchen chair since it was the only other place to sit.

We hear a lot said these days about lack of communication between the generations but I doubt if youngsters nowadays can imagine the almost total lack of communication which illiteracy can inflict. My grandmother and George could not read newspapers, the wireless set which might have kept them in touch with events was too dear for them to buy and so they had absolutely nothing to talk about except local gossip or the small happenings of their working days, and by night both of them were too tired, too dispirited to be interested in each other's daily routine. George would stare into space, smoking his evil-smelling old clay pipe, and Gran would sew in silence until it was time to retire. Often I would go out even if I had nowhere to go just to avoid these dull deadly silent evenings round the kitchen fire.

I would go sometimes to Spiritualist meetings hoping I might get some message to tell me how to set about serving humanity, but in those days there was never any message for me and since the other older members of the congregation did not speak to me or try to be friendly I was not able to contact any group of people with whom I might sit to develop my mediumship as I had been told to do in the letters from Munich. I began to be very depressed and to wonder if the letters could possibly have been some kind of elaborate hoax, but I kept returning to the fact that the woman in Munich could not possibly in any ordinary way have learned the name and address of a totally unimportant young man in a small English town, and even if she had been able to do so what on earth would be the point in playing a complicated joke on a total stranger whose reaction you would never see. I got very broody pondering on these matters and my grandmother offered to dose me with sulphur and syrup which was her panacea for all ills. I turned down the sulphur and syrup which I loathed and decided I must snap out of it by my own efforts so I made up my mind to take up dancing again.

Miss Florence said she was delighted to see me, she had been doing so well in recent months she was hardly able to cope with all the pupils who wanted to enrol. It seemed England had gone dance mad, young, middle-aged and old all wanted to be in the swim and learn to do the quickstep, the tango, the new waltz, the blackbottom and the rest. It was agreed I would help with slow learners and new pupils in return for private lessons from Miss Florence.

I went back to dancing with all the enthusiasm of a stranded fish returned to water. I practised steps in the shop between jobs, I practised in our bedroom under George's jaundiced eye, I waltzed and tango-ed through my grandmother's lines of washing in our kitchen and when I wasn't dancing with my feet I was working out routines in my head. Miss Florence said if I persevered I might even make a career in dancing and I was thrilled.

The manager's assistant at the shop was unexpectedly transferred to another branch of the firm and the manager offered me his job. Not only did I get a rise in pay to 15s a week but I would be allowed a black coat and pin-stripe trousers at cost price to wear in the shop.

Despite my rise in status I still had to sweep out, polish and dust the shop in the morning and clean the show windows as before, but when I had finished these tasks I would slip into the back shop and change from my overalls into my smart shop suit in which I felt no end of a dude. I was also allowed a discount on clothes I bought from the shop and I was allowed to pay by instalments. In this way I was able in time to get together a wardrobe. I bought two suits, a dark blue serge and, to express my more dashing self, a plum-coloured worsted. I bought a pair of the new wide flannel trousers known as Oxford bags and a tweed jacket, the two together cost me under £2, and then I got a raincoat which set me back 25s. Thus accoutred I reckoned I was quite a dandy. Each time I brought home some new item my grandmother would remark pointedly that clothes never yet made the man, but secretly she was very proud of my new image and she spent hours sponging, pressing and steaming so that I should always be immaculate. George never to my knowledge wore anything but his working corduroys and a blue-striped union shirt with a neckerchief, and he regarded my pretensions with sardonic amusement because I fell so far short of what he called real gentry, and the first time I wore my plum-coloured confection he lay on the old horsehair sofa in the kitchen and laughed until he cried.

After I had been with Miss Florence as pupil-teacher for some months a girl joined the class who I thought was a natural born dancer. Her name was Gladys and she was small, slim and lissom as a dryad, with brown hair and big hazel eyes. Her clothes were of the simple elegant kind which I suspected must cost a great deal. We liked each other from the beginning and our steps suited so well I was sure I had found the ideal partner I had dreamed about for so long. As soon as I plucked up enough courage I asked her to go to one of the local dances with me and to my joy she accepted the invitation.

On the big night, wearing my blue serge and my most tasteful tie, I arrived outside the front door of the address Gladys had given me and my heart sank into my gleaming shoes. This was the home of wealthy and important people whose daughter was far beyond my poor reach. However, I rang the bell thinking I would at least have that night to remember before her wrathful parents gave me the heave-ho. The door was opened by a maidservant in black and white trim, and I asked nervously if Miss Gladys was ready to accompany me to the dance. The maid giggled, then quickly controlled herself. 'Round the side door and ring the bell,' she said abruptly and closed the door in my face. I walked round the house to the side door wondering if the curt behaviour of the servant was the first sign of parental disapproval, and pressed the bell. Gladys wearing a white fur jacket over a flame-coloured evening gown opened the door to me. 'Cook might give us a sherry if she is in the mood, so come in,' said this vision, and I was ushered into a kitchen where a lady with a red face wearing a white coat with egg spilt on the lapels poured out two schooners of sherry from a decanter labelled 'Cooking' and handed one each to Gladys and me. Over the sherry which even my untutored palate found lacking in finesse, I learned Gladys was the upstairs maid in this imposing residence and artlessly she confided that her elegant clothes were cast-offs handed down to her by the two daughters of the family who employed her. What with the relief of finding Gladys was not after all out of reach and the unaccustomed drink which had gone straight to my head, I left the house with Gladys on my arm and walked an inch above the ground all the way to the dance-hall.

Dancing with Gladys was to know the bliss of the perfect partner, she was light as thistledown in my arms and she followed my every lead unerringly as we glided effortlessly over the floor in tune with each other and with the occasion. By the end of the evening we were already planning our future as professional ballroom dancers. We thought we might first make our names in cabaret or by winning one of the big competitions, then we would open a school together and make our fortunes. We agreed to practise together every minute we could spare and we would go as a couple to all the local dances not only to try out variations on all the latest steps to decent bands but so that we might get known in the district as expert dancers, which might lead to invitations to give exhibition

Leslie, aged 4, with his mother and father

Dr Louis Young, the scientist, with Edith and Leslie at St Albans in 1935

Owen, Edith and Leslie on holiday in 1936

dances or even to cabaret offers. Gladys and I especially enjoyed dancing the tango and on this, our first public appearance so to speak, our version of this beautiful dance pleased the crowd hanging around the dance floor so much that they applauded and demanded an encore, just as I had dreamed might happen if ever I found a partner like Gladys. Few people learn to dance the tango well; they may master the steps and even feel its rhythm, but to do real justice to it one must have the right temperament and most English people are too stiff and too inhibited to let themselves go in the romantic sensuality which is its true meaning.

When I left Gladys at the side door of her employers' mansion in the small hours we were already in imagination a world-famous dance team and we renewed our promises to work hard and often with kisses.

In the weeks which followed we went to all the dances we could find and, according to plan, we became well known in the district as experts and we grew accustomed to applause and to graciously acceding to requests for an encore. Our personal relationship remained on the level of our ambitions, but often moments which might have grown into tenderness were inhibited by Gladys' insistence that she was not 'that kind of a girl' and she wanted none of 'that' before her marriage lines were safely signed, sealed and delivered into her hand. The mere mention of marriage was like a cold douche to me. I remembered only too clearly the misery and discord in the seedy furnished room which had been my parents' home. But Gladys and I got on well enough and to dance with her was sheer delight.

In the autumn of 1931 a local charity planned to hold a fund-raising dance in the largest hall in St Albans and the organisers asked Gladys and me to appear in the midnight cabaret without a fee as our contribution to the cause. We were so sure this was the first rung on the ladder to fame and fortune we accepted with alacrity. We decided to dance our tango, by now a dramatised version with added steps of our own invention, and to follow it with a quickstep if we were asked for an encore. At this point Gladys revealed an unexpected propensity for managing and she announced we would wear Spanish costumes for the tango and I must chip in my share of the cost of materials and she would run them up on the Singer sewing machine at the house where she worked. It seemed to me time spent in sewing costumes would be better employed in practising our act but Gladys was determined we would make a dramatic impact and so I handed over my money. After discussions which seemed endless on the merits of various materials Gladys contrived two very striking costumes, though I am bound to say I was not too happy about the Cordoban hat she found for me to wear with mine. I was already conscious of being too short for professional dancing and I felt the hat would extinguish me completely, but Gladys was determined I would wear it and I wore it.

We were a terrific success on the big night and we finished our exhibition to prolonged, ear-splitting applause which was music in our ears and to acknowledge which I thankfully removed The Hat. As Gladys gracefully curtseyed and I bowed to the non-stop plaudits both of us felt we only had to reach out and the career we wanted would be ours.

Some weeks after this almost professional début Gladys and I were out walking when we passed a big old Victorian house in a residential part of the town. The house belonged to two elderly sisters who kept a nursery school for children under five called The Hall Nursery School, but in those days women did not commonly work outside their homes and help in the nursery was readily available and cheap, and so the demand for establishments in which to dump burdensome tots was not so great as it is today and I imagine the Hall School was rather less than a resounding financial success. At all events, on this day there was a hand-printed notice pinned to one of the trees offering the school assembly hall for hire in the evenings at a reasonable fee for parties, lectures, soirées. Gladys and I stopped in our tracks, both struck by the same thrilling

66

idea. Gladys' hazel eyes were dancing with excitement. 'No harm in asking, is there?' she said, and we walked through the gateway.

I tugged the old-fashioned bell-pull and somewhere behind the massive front door the bell clanged. Shortly the door was opened by a quiet little mouse of a lady dressed in grey silk who looked at us interrogatively without speaking. When we told her we wanted to ask about hiring the hall she thought we had better see her sister. We followed her upright back into a room which was evidently a play-room for the tots. There was a dapple-grey rocking-horse with splendid scarlet nostrils and a long tail standing in one corner, and other toys could be seen neatly stacked in an open cupboard. The elder sister, her hair in a frenzy, was painting a play-pen with white paint. She looked up as the grey mouse sister ushered us into the room, she had a smudge of paint on the end of her nose. I asked politely if we could see the assembly hall with a view to hiring it on two evenings a week to teach ballroom dancing. The older lady remarked inconsequentially that they did not seem to dance the gavotte or the lancers much nowadays, but she supposed cats could look at kings. Miss Mouse seemed to take this last remark as permission for us to view the hall and she invited us to follow her.

Gladys and I surveyed the parquet floor of what had once been the gracious drawing-room of the house and, in spite of the damage patterings of tiny feet had caused in the way of scratches and scuff marks, we nodded our satisfaction to each other. The room was ideal for our purpose. There was even a grand piano in the window bay and an old cabinet gramophone standing against the wall. Miss Mouse agreed that the gramophone was included in the hire but said we must bring our own needles and be responsible for any damage to the machine. We thought this was fair and said we would call again when we knew on which nights we needed the hall, then we bid Miss Mouse good afternoon and went away to talk things over.

I was officially Gladys' 'follower' by now and sometimes the cook would give me a meal in the kitchen on nights when Gladys was housebound. On one such occasion when the table was cleared Gladys and I concocted a brochure to advertise the Hall School of Dancing, Principals: L. Flint and G. Hayes. Our charges were one guinea for a course of five private lessons from one of the Principals and two shillings per person per evening for the open class. Later we found a back street printer who ran off a thousand handbills from our copy and we both spent hours of our spare time distributing these to factories and leaving them carelessly on shop counters or pushing them through the letter-boxes of houses. Before too long the Hall School of Dancing actually had pupils and if we only had two people taking the guinea course we sometimes had as many as twenty in the open class. We had a problem with the music. The gramophone was wheezy and ancient and we had very few records so we spent so much time changing them from side to side and winding the gramophone that pupils were complaining they did not get their two bob's worth of tuition because of the constant pauses to deal with the elderly gramophone. We began to look around for someone to play the piano in return for the small fee we could offer, but without any success.

One morning I was on the step-ladder outside the shop polishing the show windows and doubtless thinking up new dance routines when a woman called to me from the pavement. I came down from the steps to see who she was and recognised a lady who had sometimes acted as librarian at the Spiritualist church in the days when I was going there. She introduced herself as Mrs Mundin and said she had not seen me at the church for so long she felt she had to speak to me when she saw me on the steps. I thought she was probably in her early forties but still very attractive, with a gaiety of manner which I found pleasing. I told her I had completely lost interest in Spiritualism and my time was taken up trying to make a career for myself. 'What a pity,' said Mrs Mundin, 'I heard you were showing signs of quite outstanding medium-ship in Mrs Cook's home circle.' Though it had happened so long before, yet I still felt myself turn scarlet at the memory of my disastrous final appearance in Mrs Cook's circle. 'I don't want to be a medium,' I said firmly, 'it seems a rotten kind of life to me.' Mrs Mundin looked sad and said it was a shame to waste a gift when there were so very few good mediums. I answered that I probably wasn't any good anyway and I was too busy with this world to trouble about the next. Mrs Mundin's level grey eyes disapproved of me. 'If you have a gift, it is your duty to develop it and use it,' she said. 'I am starting a home circle and I would be happy if you would join us.' Not wanting to appear churlish, I smiled kindly as I shook my head. 'Come to tea on Sunday and meet my friends,' persisted the soft pretty voice, 'we will have tea and talk, then perhaps I will play the piano.' I pricked up my ears. 'Do you play dance music or the other kind?' I inquired brashly. When Mrs Mundin said she played both kinds I accepted her invitation.

The minute I set foot in Mrs Mundin's pretty little drawing-room it was obvious to me she and her friends were far above my station in life and at first I was paralysed with shyness and feelings of inferiority which the silver tea service and the delicate cups and saucers on the tea-trolley did nothing to dispel. Fortunately for me Mrs Mundin and her friends had that true gentility which never discomforts those who have been less privileged than themselves and before long I found them as easy and relaxed as old shoes. After a delicious tea Mrs Mundin, by then I was calling her Edith, played Chopin, Brahms and Bach and I had to admit to myself that these hitherto shunned gentlemen appealed to me in a way I would never have expected. Then to please me, Edith played all the latest dance tunes with such skill that my feet itched to dance. This was my first experience of a home where the criterion of acceptance was not who you were or where you came from but what kind of human being you were, and I knew instinctively that despite my uncertain grammar, my poverty and my lack of education these people accepted me as one of themselves and they liked me. I wanted to see more of them and so when the question of the circle came up I agreed to sit with them every Wednesday evening, which was the one evening which would not interfere with any of my other activities. Even so as I walked home I wondered if I had been wise to start up all that spirit business again and I was determined not to let it interfere with my efforts to build up the Hall School of Dancing with Gladys. That reminded me that Gladys would probably be pretty scathing about the idea of me developing as a medium. I decided discretion was the better part of valour and I would keep my own counsel.

I need hardly have worried on either score because though I sat regularly every Wednesday evening in Edith's circle for many weeks absolutely nothing happened so far as any development of my psychic powers was concerned, and I came to the conclusion that if I ever had any such powers they had left me for ever. I would not have regretted this except for the disappointment it must be to the other members of the circle who had heard such tales of my wonderful mediumship from members of Mrs Cook's circle, but in all the long succession of blank evenings not one member of the circle ever made me feel I had not come up to their expectations and I began to feel a warm genuine affection for each one of them. While we were sitting together as a circle I could actually feel a warm tide of affection flowing from them towards me and these blank evenings were rewarding in the quiet joy of repose, tranquillity and friendship shared. What I did not realise until long afterwards was that during the months when nothing seemed to be happening we ourselves were creating the very conditions of harmony and love in which the gift of mediumship can flower best.

Gladys and I still had problems with our music, we had not found anyone who would play the piano for us at the very small fee we could offer and we struggled on with the gramophone, but we lost many pupils because of the long pauses caused by coping with the elderly machine. When Edith heard about our difficulty she at once offered to play for us on two nights a week and although I knew she was having money worries herself at this time she refused to accept any fee. Gladys had become very possessive and I was apprehensive about her reaction to Edith but the fact that we had acquired a first-class pianist for nothing outweighed her fear of losing me. Gladys went down considerably in my estimation when after Edith had left for home at their first meeting, she said bitchily, 'Your lady friend is well past it, isn't she?'

One night when our circle was sitting as usual suddenly the whole room seemed to grow icy cold and rush away from me and I lost consciousness. When I returned to a normal waking state I learned that various entities had spoken through me including Edith's late husband who had been the brother of Herbert Mundin the well-known comedy star.

As months passed our circle became an ever more harmonious group. Sometimes I would be entranced and discarnate persons would speak through me. At first these were relatives and friends of the other members of the circle, but that phase passed after a long period of time and spiritually progressed beings from the other side began to speak through me on matters of philosophy and ethics. Edith would write down all that transpired while I was in trance and when I returned to waking consciousness I would marvel at the learned discourses and the cultured language which had come through my lips.

After a further long period of months a new facet of my mediumship developed and I became clairvoyant. I could see and describe the spirit people who gathered round us during our sittings. As I saw them they were as solid and lifelike as any other member of the group but they had the same disconcerting habit of vanishing abruptly as the people I had seen as a child.

Eventually Edith's money problems became so acute she

had to give up her little house because she could no longer afford the rent and she and her son Owen, a bright attractive child of nine, moved into a council house on the outskirts of St Albans and Edith took a job trimming hats in a local factory. But during this time of change and disruption there was no break in the regular sitting of our circle, the meeting place was changed to the house of the two other members so that the development of my mediumship would not suffer any check.

On the nights when I was not sitting with the circle I still went to local dances with Gladys or taught in our school, and Gladys became ever more suspicious because I would never see her on Wednesday nights however desirable a dance was being held and she openly began to demand what was the attraction which made Wednesday evening sacrosanct. I knew very well she would either laugh at me or nag unbearably to try and make me give up the circle so I never told her anything more than that it was my own business.

My gallivantings with Gladys were also causing trouble with my grandmother. In spite of the fact I was twenty-two years of age she still refused to allow me a front door key of my own. This meant that when I was out late dancing either she sat up to let me into the house, which she did with the air of an affronted archangel, or she would go to bed and I would have to throw pebbles up at George's window to waken him out of his beery stupor to come down and open the door. I hardly knew which alternative was the more grisly, but the situation certainly led to many exacerbating rows in our house. I began to dread going home from work to face an embattled grandmother or a flow of invective from George, or even a concerted attack by both.

Edith was not very happy at this time either, she had moved far away from the friends and neighbours on whom she had been used to rely for company and she had made no new friends among her neighbours on the council estate who resented her superior education and her more intellectual interests. Apart from Wednesday nights when the circle met she was very lonely, and I formed the habit of dropping in to see her and young Owen on nights when I had no other engagement, rather than stay at home in the grim atmosphere generated by my grandmother and George. Edith was always flatteringly pleased to see me and she always had time and patience to listen to my problems and to give me advice and comfort. I liked Owen very much too, and I began to look on him as the young brother I had never had, and I think he grew quite fond of me. I remember one Boxing Day Edith and I planned a treat for him. We pooled our money and took the early train to London where we queued for the Pit at the Drury Lane Theatre and after a long wait we got in to see the marvellous pantomime which the theatre used to present every Christmas. After the show we ate at a Lyons' Corner House to the accompaniment of a string orchestra before returning to St Albans on a late train. We had a glorious outing and the total cost for the three of us was no more than 30s.

I did not know it any more than did the other members of our circle but my development as a medium was entering its last and most important phase. I was still very much a film fan and I would go to the cinema as often as I could to see the talkies to which I had now become quite reconciled, but every time I was sitting in the comfortable dark of the cinema my eyes glued to the screen I became aware of strange whisperings going on around me, I could catch only an odd word here and there but the voices were those of both men and women and it was made very clear to me that other members of the audience could also hear them because I was constantly being told to shut up or thumped angrily on the back by those sitting behind me. I would protest that I had not opened my mouth but as the whisperings continued and more and more people began to complain, I would eventually crawl unhappily out of the cinema without seeing the film. This happened so often that I had to give up going to the cinema altogether. I now know it was the earliest manifestation of the voice mediumship which was to bring me fame, if not fortune, and that it was made possible by the fact that I was sitting in the darkness of the auditorium surrounded by many people whose minds were concentrated on the screen to the exclusion of random or distracting thoughts, but at the time it puzzled me and deprived me of one of my greatest pleasures.

Things at home got more unpleasant. I would not give up my late night dancing and my grandmother adamantly refused to hand over a latch key, and the constant discord in the house made me moody, depressed and miserable. Edith came to my rescue and offered to turn her boxroom into a bedroom for me if I would care to be her lodger at a rent of a few shillings a week to include breakfast before I went to work. And so without regret on either side I left my grandmother's house which had been my home for so many years and moved into Edith's council house as her paying guest. Under Edith's care and in the peace of her home I grew happier and more contented and doubtless because of the greater harmony within myself the development of my voice mediumship accelerated and we began to get the voices in our circle sittings. At first more of the confused whisperings, later strong clear voices who announced themselves as the persons they had been on earth, giving their names and addresses and telling us about their lives on earth. To my joy I was not now taken into trance while these manifestations took place, I, too, could hear and appreciate everything that went on in the circle. Indeed I could even hold intelligent conversations with some of the spirit entities who were able to manifest through my mediumship and I can still do so today.

For a long time after this acceleration of my development in the circle I had been torn between my desire for a career as a professional dancer with Gladys and the constant urging by spirit entities that I must give up everything to serve and comfort humanity through my mediumship. I still hankered after the lights and the applause of a professional dancer's life and I simply could not make up my mind to give up the idea altogether. For a long time I tried to get the best of both worlds in a literal sense and while Wednesday night was reserved for the 'other side', the other nights of the week were devoted to furthering the ambitions of Gladys and myself.

I was wandering down the main street in St Albans one Saturday afternoon window-shopping, making my way among the housewives and paterfamiliases doing their week-end buying. There seemed to be more people about even than usual on Saturday and I was pleased rather than otherwise to see Gladys walking towards me through the crowds, although lately she and I had had many quarrels because of her possessive jealousy which had grown almost pathological. I stopped to greet her and I was smiling as it crossed my mind to ask her to go for a bus ride into the country and I would try as hard as I could to give her a happy and carefree day. She stopped in front of me and before I could get out words of greeting she slapped me as hard as she could across the face, shouting as she did so that I was living with that woman old enough to be my mother. Having delivered this bombshell she turned on her heel and stalked out of my life for ever.

As I stood in the middle of the pavement red with embarrassment, my face stinging from Gladys' wallop, I was horribly conscious of the amused, scornful or sympathetic stares from the crowds who had not been so entertained on a Saturday shopping trip for many a long day. Suddenly I knew a blinding conviction that from now on I would give up any thought of a career as a dancer. I knew there was something far more important I had to do with my life. I would give all my life, all my gifts and all my devotion to serving my fellow men and to proving through my mediumship the glorious, comforting truth of man's survival of his bodily death.

Six

ONE night when our circle was meeting on the usual evening, something happened which convinced me beyond all doubt that I had made the right decision.

The six of us were sitting together in the quiet darkness, when a man's voice began to speak to us in a foreign language. We listened to him without understanding a word. Finally Edith ventured tentatively, 'I am not certain but I think it might be Italian.' 'Si, signora,' said the spirit voice, 'Italian was my mother tongue when I was on earth but I knew some English too and I will speak so that you may all understand. My name was Valentino and I have come tonight to say how happy I am that this young man has at last accepted the life path he must tread and I want to tell him that one day when he is a famous medium he will hold a seance in the room which was my bedroom in my house in Hollywood and I will come to speak to him there when he does so.' At last, after all the messages from the various mediums, after all the letters from Munich, Valentino had spoken to me in his own voice through my own developed mediumship, and even if the idea of my ever reaching Hollywood seemed preposterous at the time, his message filled me with joy and the desire to use my gift to help people.

From that night onwards Edith began with great tact and gentleness to educate me for the public work she knew I must do. She would ask me to read to her, then she would correct my grammar and my pronunciation. She taught me table manners and many of the small courtesies and refinements which would make it easier for me to feel confident when I had to be in the public eye and meet people of all kinds. Many times I must have jarred on her unbearably because of my ignorance and the uncouthness of my manners, but she never let me know it and slowly, with infinite kindness, she changed me from the country lad I was into a man acceptable on most levels of society. She opened out before me a new world of books, music and art, she made life a richer and fuller experience than it could ever have been without her. I owed her so much more than I could ever repay.

Some months after Valentino had spoken at our circle Edith greeted me one evening when I came home from work with the extraordinary news that the medium of a small local Spiritualist church had eloped with a member of his congregation and the church committee had invited me to take his place on the platform at the next service. I wondered if I were ready to speak and demonstrate in public, in fact the very idea frightened me to death, but Edith said I must have complete trust in the spiritual beings who used me as a channel in our circle and I agreed to take the place of the missing medium.

On the day of the service which was to be my first public work as a medium, Edith and I went along to the church an hour before the time of the service with the idea of arranging flowers in vases for the platform. As we arrived outside the church with our arms full of flowers and leaves we were startled to see two men loading chairs into a van standing outside the entrance. In the church we learned from a distracted member of the committee that the chairs were being repossessed by the firm who had supplied them because the hire purchase payments were so heavily in arrears. The thought of a service where not only the congregation but those on the platform including the medium had to stand throughout because there was nothing to sit on was hardly encouraging. A diligent search of our resources by Edith and me yielded thirty-odd shillings between us and we went out to offer this to the men if they would leave the chairs for one more night. The men sympathised with our dilemma but they told us they must have the full amount owing or take the chairs. I was standing on the pavement disconsolately watching the last of the chairs disappear into the maw of the pantechnicon when a big friendly hand clapped me on the shoulder. 'Nay, lad, no need to be down in t'mouth. Ah'll not let them tak' the chairs from under ye.' I turned to see Mr Whittaker, a bluff kindly Yorkshireman who with his wife had sat in Mrs Cook's circle. 'Ah allus knew ye had it in ye, lad, and ah'm giving ye t'chance to show it.' Mr Whittaker, bless him, pulled out his cheque book and soon the chairs were being carted back into the church.

As soon as I stepped to the edge of the platform that night to speak I felt the familiar sensation of the room rushing away from me and I lost consciousness of my surroundings. When I woke from the trance an hour later I learned that I had delivered a most interesting discourse and followed it by a brilliant demonstration of clairvoyance while under the control of a spirit who introduced himself as White Wing, who was one of the spiritually evolved entities who often controlled me in our circle before my independent direct voice mediumship developed. Since it was not possible for the voices to manifest in a fully lighted hall White Wing clearly had come to help me out in this first public appearance by taking control of me in trance.

After the meeting closed various members of the congregation crowded round me to tell me about the wonderful proofs they had been given that the dead lived on in another plane of being and had not ceased to care for those they had left behind them. As I saw the happiness which shone out of the faces of those who told me their stories of the way in which husband, father, son or mother had proved his or her continuing existence I felt humble and deeply grateful to have been used to bring such joy.

That night Edith and I sat up late talking over the events at the meeting and we both agreed that if my trance mediumship could bring such comfort to the bereaved, how much more convincing proof could be given to them if they were able to talk to their loved ones and hear them reply by means of my independent direct voice mediumship. We both knew that to offer this comfort to the people we must open a mission of our own where we could provide the darkened room which the average Spiritualist church does not require, since trance mediumship or clairvoyance which one normally presents in Spiritualist churches can be given in full light. It is only physical mediumship, materialisation, apportation or the direct voice which need to be conducted in complete darkness. We would need at least some capital and I would have to give up my job. We talked long and late about this possibility and before we went to bed we decided to save every penny in the hope that one day we would have enough behind us to open a church of our own.

After the successful meeting at the local church I began to be invited to take meetings at other churches outside the area in which I lived and gradually I became known and my services in demand throughout the whole of Hertfordshire, but always I cherished the dream of our own mission and I saved to make it a reality.

One Sunday afternoon Edith and I were relaxing in front of the fire after what I had learned to call luncheon when I saw Edith who was looking out of the window turn white and bite her lip as if something had vexed her. When I asked her what was wrong she told me her parents were outside with the obvious intention of ringing our bell.

Edith was fond of her parents but she had long since grown away from the rigid orthodoxy of their religious beliefs and she much resented their intolerance of Spiritualism, of the truth of which she had been convinced long before I met her. In common with most psychics I am rarely vouchsafed any premonition of a personal disaster and that Sunday was no exception to the rule. I rose to greet Edith's parents when she ushered them into the sitting-room with the ingenuous friendliness of a dog wagging its tail. Beaming a big welcome at them both, I held out my hand to her father. To my astonishment he struck it from him as though it were some species of poisonous serpent and embarked on a tirade against Spiritualism in general and mediums in particular the imaginative invective of which I have never heard equalled since, and yet every word he said could have been uttered with perfect propriety in the most genteel of drawing-rooms. First, he castigated me for what he called dabbling and delving into the Devil's own mysteries, then he painted a vivid word picture of the somewhat specialised torments which awaited me in Hell hereafter for allowing myself to be used by evil and personating spirits whose only aim was to seduce souls from the light. I listened to him open-mouthed, I had never before heard this view of the gentle philosophy in which I believe. I could hardly believe my own ears. When Edith tried to stem her father's flow of denunciation he turned on her and to the astonishment of both of us accused her with many an Old Testament epithet of living with me in sin and lechery. When I attempted to intervene to point out both the injustice and the inaccuracy of this attack I merely drew down on my reeling head a new fusillade of invective. When the patriarch had exhausted both his thunder and himself he gathered up his more introvert lady and swept her out of the abode of the wicked where defilement dwelt.

When they had gone I dried Edith's tears and tried to comfort her and as I did so it was suddenly blindingly obvious to me that I truly loved this kind and gentle lady who was my friend, my teacher, my confidante and the centre of my life. Then and there I begged her to marry me. She refused even to think of it because of the difference in our ages, and the more I pleaded with her the more adamant she became, and, on that occasion at least, I gave up trying to persuade her.

At long last the day came when we thought we had saved

up enough to start our own Mission. I gave in my notice at John Maxwell's shop and while I was working out my fort-night's warning I found a large unfurnished room over a shop in nearby Watford, which I rented for a very few shillings a week, though my courage almost failed me at the thought of taking on even so small a commitment when I would soon be without a job. Edith and I spent all our free time painting, staining and polishing the bare floor boards and making cur-tains, and when we had installed a couple of dozen chairs, bought on hire purchase, the somewhat dreary room in a Wat-ford side street had been transformed into a pleasant and com-fortable church. Finally, an advertisement in the local paper announced that the Watford Spiritualist Mission had opened its doors.

However long I may live, whatever is left for me to enjoy, nothing can ever equal the thrill of my first service in my own church. Every seat was filled and latecomers crowded at the back of the room. I was taken into trance for the address and for the clairvoyance and when I returned to the waking state the feeling of joy and lightness I sensed in that crowded room was indescribable and the weeks of hard work, the penny-pinching and the anxieties were all worth while.

We went on as we had started and very soon we had to buy more chairs while we were still paying off the instalments on the first lot. Needless to say the second purchase of chairs was also on easy terms because, in spite of the numbers who came to the Mission, they were for the most part people who were almost as hard up as I was myself and there was barely enough in the collections we took at the services to pay rent, lighting, heating and the instalments on two lots of chairs. For my own living expenses I relied on private seances for direct voice which I held once a week in the sitting-room of Edith's council house and for which I charged one guinea for two persons.

I wanted those who could not attend private seances either because they could not afford them or because they were at work during the time they were held, to have this experience which, I think, of all forms of mediumship, gives the most convincing proof of man's survival of his bodily death and so Edith and I decided to hold what we called an open circle after our usual service on Thursday evenings. When the service was over and the congregation had dispersed to their homes a few people who had booked a seat for two shillings would remain behind and we would sit in darkness and people whom the world calls dead would come to talk to us. My voice mediumship by this time was almost fully developed and more often than not I was fully conscious during these group seances and perforce had to listen to all that was said both by living members of the circle and their friends and relations from the other side of life. Sometimes the talks between them were so intimate and so charged with emotion I would feel like an eavesdropper. On one occasion a man's voice said he wanted to speak to his son George and he was answered by a man sitting in the circle. The discarnate father proceeded to take the living son to task for his extravagance and begged him to cut down his drinking and to be kinder and more considerate to Anne. When the circle was closed and people were leaving for home a lady and gentleman lingered behind to talk to me. The man introduced himself and I learned he was a famous film director. He told me he was completely convinced he had been speaking to his dead father not only because no one else in the world had ever called him George, which was not his baptismal name, but because the content of the little lecture and the mannerisms of speech were typical of his father in life. Bringing forward the lady with him he introduced me to his wife, Anne.

On another of these Thursday open circle meetings after various friends and relatives had spoken in the usual way we heard a woman's voice trying to speak to us, in the uncertain way in which new communicators sometimes manifest. Eventually her voice became stronger though she sounded distressed. She told us she was Lucy Doris Covell who had lived in St Albans Road, Watford, she was a secretary who had been murdered, and her body had not yet been found. Her voice faded and one of the entities who guide me from the other side came through to tell us the girl was distressed at the manner of her passing and very worried about the man who had killed her who was her lover and less to blame for what had happened than she was herself. Naturally we watched the local paper after this sitting to see if the facts the girl had given us about herself would be verified and only a few days later we read that the girl's body had been discovered and the man she had been living with had disappeared. At our next open circle the murdered girl returned to speak to us and though she was calmer she was still concerned about her lover who had not yet been found by the police. She told us that on the night of her death her lover had been out on his own and when he came home in the small hours he wakened her and they had a furious row. She had said angry and bitter things which goaded him beyond endurance and he hit out at her with the bicycle pump he had in his hand. He had not meant to do her any serious injury but because of a physical abnormality of her own the blow killed her. Because the lover was terrified no one would believe his story, foolishly he ran away. The girl said the police would find him sitting in a local park playing with a piece of string trying to find the courage to take his own life. A day or so later we read in the local paper that the man had been found and arrested in just the way the girl had described. He was sent for trial on a charge of murder and during the trial the girl returned to speak several times. Each time she came she told us with great confidence her lover would not be found guilty of her murder, the charge would be reduced to one of manslaughter and he would be sentenced to five years in prison and in the event this is what happened. Since the lover may well be still living and his debt to society was paid a long time ago it would not be just to re-open a matter which must have caused him great suffering by mentioning his name in this book but there must be many people in the Watford area who remember the seances where the dead girl told her story, and the story of her death and her lover's trial were fully reported in the local paper at the time.

One night at another of my open circles a woman from the other side of life spoke to a man sitting with the group and said she was his first wife who had been burned to death in a fire at their factory. She told him she wanted him to know how happy she was that he had married her younger sister and she was glad they had so much enjoyed their honeymoon in Brazil. This man stayed behind after the seance was over to tell me how impressed he was with the demonstration of my mediumship he had been given and to ask if he could speak to me privately on a matter of great importance. I agreed to accompany him to a nearby café where we could talk over a cup of coffee.

In the café I learned my friend was Mr Noah Zerdin, one of the founders and now the head of The Link Association of Home Circles. The object of this organisation was to bring together as many members of Spiritualist home circles throughout the world as possible to exchange experiences they had in their circles and to provide a common meeting ground for people of like interests.

I was most interested to learn about Mr Zerdin's work with The Link but I sat up with a jerk in my café chair when he asked me if I was aware I was risking my life every time I held one of my open circles for the direct voice. I suppose I looked as incredulous as I felt, for Mr Zerdin went on to explain to me how dangerous it was to allow any Tom, Dick or Harry from the streets to attend these seances. He told me that at such times there exuded from me a life force called ectoplasm by means of which the voices of the spirit people could manifest and if any person in the circle through malice or mere curiosity shone a bright light on me this life force would rush back into my body with such violence that would at best cause me a violent shock, at worst internal haemorrhage and death. I gaped at him, I simply could not imagine that people who were being helped and comforted by my mediumship

84

would want to harm me. There would always be those who doubted the genuineness of the phenomena Mr Zerdin explained and they would consider they were acting in the interests of others if they tried to expose some medium whose powers were attracting a following. I protested that surely common sense must tell such people it was impossible for me to know the intimate details of other people's lives of which the voices spoke nor could I by any stretch of the imagination speak in the hundreds of voices and accents, both male and female, which were heard at my seances. Mr Zerdin persisted in warning me that many people were deeply prejudiced against the phenomena of Spiritualism, either because of religious bigotry or because of intellectual convictions of a nihilist nature, and such people would welcome the opportunity to create a disturbance at seances like mine and would think nothing of the possible harm which might be caused to the medium, even if they knew enough about the subject to know the damage they might inflict. Mr Zerdin went on to say mediumship such as mine was so rare I must preserve it, treasure it, protect it so that as many as possible might be blessed by it. He suggested I should sit regularly for a while in his own home circle, each member of which was highly experienced in psychic science, and during these sittings the circle as a whole would concentrate exclusively on the greater development of my mediumship. Then when the time was ripe they would consider how best to bring me out of obscurity to serve in a wider and more public field where instead of convincing a mere handful of people in my little mission I could spread the truth of man's survival of death to thousands.

Going home in the bus that night I thought over everything Mr Zerdin had said. Noah Zerdin was then, and at eighty years of age he is still, a most impressive man. I had been deeply moved by his burning sincerity and the compassion which urged him to share his own conviction with as many people as possible. Apparently he had been an atheist for many years before his own conviction of survival had come to change his life for the better and he was filled with the desire to help humanity as he had been helped. By the time I got home I had made up my mind not only to take his advice to be more careful about the bona fides of those who sat with me in my open circles but also to accept his suggestion to sit in his circle for the greater development of my powers.

For many months after that night I sat regularly in Noah's circle, which was held in the pleasant house in Merton Park where he lived with his delightful wife Goldie. Because of the unselfish and devoted way in which the Zerdin circle concentrated their thoughts and prayers on me, the voices greatly increased in strength.

I still carried on my work at the Mission during these months though I cut down my open circles owing to a new commitment with Noah's Link organisation to hold small groups for the members in conditions where my mediumship could operate properly. I also continued to hold my weekly seance in Edith's house when she was at work and Owen was at school, in order to earn the guinea which was my livelihood.

One afternoon I was standing at the window of Edith's sitting-room looking out for a Miss M. Tucker who had booked an appointment with me by letter. Suddenly my eyes popped out of my head like two organ stops as an immaculate Rolls-Royce pulled up outside our house and a smart chauffeur handed out a large lady whom I presumed must be Miss M. Tucker. Cars like this one were hardly thick on the ground in our council estate and the large lady's progress to our front door was followed with passionate interest by neighbours standing on their doorsteps or peering from behind curtains. I opened the door when the bell rang to learn the lady was indeed Miss Tucker and she turned out to be a very nice person with none of the disdainful airs and graces I had feared the owner of such a splendid motor-car might possess.

I ushered her into the sitting-room and when she was comfortably seated I turned off the light and the seance began.

After a few minutes the boyish Cockney voice of Mickey, the spirit helper who acts as a sort of master of ceremonies at my seances, greeted the lady and told her he was going to help her mother and her sister to speak to her. He was as good as his word and shortly Miss Tucker was having an affectionate and intimate chat with her deceased mother and sister. When these two spirits had said good-bye a man's voice was heard announcing himself as Edison and demanding to know why the lady had not brought Louis with her. They had a short conversation and Miss Tucker promised to bring Louis with her next week if the medium would give her another appointment. Naturally I was glad to do this.

At the appointed hour the following week the big Rolls again stopped outside our house and Miss Tucker got out with an elderly man. He was short, red-faced and rather jolly looking and he wore a monocle. I opened the door and Miss Tucker introduced the jolly little man as Mr Louis and we went into the sitting-room for the seance.

Miss Tucker's mother talked to her for a short while then Mickey told her her other dear ones would stand aside on this occasion because Mr Edison was very anxious to speak to Louis. Shortly the man's voice we had heard the previous week was heard. 'Hello, Louis, it's Thomas speaking.' 'Thomas?' said the little man, 'Thomas Who?'

'Don't you know me, Louis? It's Thomas Alva Edison speaking,' said the voice. 'Don't you remember when we were together in the States? Surely you haven't forgotten how we worked together, struggled together to invent things?'

Now the little man gladly greeted the spirit who called himself Thomas Alva Edison and a fascinating conversation ensued between them which I could not help but overhear. They talked about times they had enjoyed together in the past and people they had both known. I heard them refer more than once to Houdini who I later discovered was a famous escapologist who once allowed himself to be tied and chained and placed in a barrel which was sent over Niagara

Falls and lived to tell the tale. They talked about Maskelyne and Devant who according to the discarnate Edison had a regular show in St George's Hall at the turn of the century. I listened enthralled to their talk though most of the people they mentioned were unknown to me and I only found out later who they had been and what they had done.

When the seance was over and the light had been turned on again Miss Tucker confessed that the man she had introduced as Mr Louis was really her husband Dr Louis Young and he had been very friendly with Edison in the States during the eighties and nineties of the previous century. She told me Tucker was her maiden name which she still used for her business, which was The Tucker Manufacturing Company in Harlesden, but she had deliberately misled me about their names so that if any evidence came through it would be more valuable. Dr Young told me he had sat with many mediums both in this country and in America but the evidence he had received that day was incontrovertibly the best he had ever received. Because he had devised many tricks and illusions for Maskelyne and Devant in the old days it had made him very aware of the possibility of fraud, but after talking with his old friend and sharing with him their joint memories he was unable to doubt that he had been speaking to Thomas Alva Edison himself.

I was to see a great deal of Miss Tucker and her husband, they sat with me on many occasions and we became great friends. Many famous people came to talk to Dr Young who seemed to have known many of the great men of science and letters. Sir Arthur Conan Doyle, Sir Oliver Lodge and many others of the same eminence came regularly to talk with him.

After many months of sitting in the Zerdin circle Noah and the Committee of The Link decided to organise a big London meeting at which I would demonstrate my now greatly strengthened voice mediumship.

The meeting was advertised for several weeks in advance in the Spiritualist newspaper *Psychic News* and it was to take place after the fifth annual conference of The Link Association in Bloomsbury's Victoria Hall on Saturday, 16 May 1935. 'Big Direct Voice Seance, Medium Leslie Flint', said the advertisement in bold black type and my heart quailed when I saw it. How did I know, how did anyone know if the voices would come? I was not able to guarantee then any more than I can guarantee today that phenomena will occur, so why on earth, I wondered, had I allowed the enthusiasm of my sponsors to talk me into appearing in a public hall in front of hundreds of people who had paid to hear them? I did not know then, nor do I know now, what are the most favourable conditions for the voices to manifest but I began strongly to suspect that a public hall filled with hundreds of people with varying motives, different ways of thinking and in or out of harmony with each other was likely to be less than ideal. I spent days plunged in the deepest gloom anticipating failure and public humiliation and it was only Edith's gentle reminders that those who help me from the other side of life have never failed me which kept me on a sufficiently even keel to board the Green Line coach with her for the journey to London on the big day, and all the way there I kept envying the other passengers because they were not Leslie Flint on his way to London to make a fool of himself in public.

Once I was seated on the platform of the Victoria Hall, surrounded by the familiar faces of Noah and his friends, I felt somewhat more relaxed, though the people packing the auditorium seemed to be just one big menacing blur. I listened to various speeches without really hearing a word of any of them, then Noah advanced to the edge of the platform and told the blur an experiment was about to take place with a new young voice medium, Leslie Flint. My hour had struck. Noah asked for all the lights in the hall to be put out with the sole exception of the exit signs which must remain lighted to conform with public safety regulations. When this was done I was dismayed to see the hall was full of light not only from the exit signs, light was coming in from all directions and this was going to make any demonstration of my mediumship even more difficult than I had imagined. With all the optimism of Daniel entering the lions' den I sat in the chair provided for me and waited.

After a few moments those on the platform heard a voice speak very faintly, much too faintly for anyone in the audience to hear it. Someone on the platform suggested he would shield me from the light with his coat and he removed it and held it in front of me. This seemed to help because various voices were then heard which were sufficiently loud to be heard by people in the audience. I listened to various short conversations between the living and those from the other side of life but I could not help thinking how unimpressive they were compared to those which took place in my mission at Watford. A spirit voice who claimed he was Earl Jellicoe spoke to a man in the audience who immediately stood rigidly to attention. A short conversation ensued between the man and the spirit voice and when the voice faded away the man told the rest of the audience he had served under Jellicoe in the Navy and what had been said was very evidential. There were a few more attempts at communication which I thought very poor, then the voices faded out and the meeting was closed.

Although the demonstration was by no means the total disaster I had feared it might be, I was deeply disappointed with the results which had been achieved and so I was all the more amazed when the audience gave me a long round of applause before I left the platform. I found this embarrassing because I did not feel the demonstration deserved such enthusiasm and I could not help thinking how these generous people would appreciate the happenings in the Watford Mission. Glad the ordeal was over, Edith and I slipped out by a side door to find somewhere we could have a meal.

At the next meeting of the Zerdin circle we had a long discussion as to how we could overcome the light problem in public demonstrations because total darkness is really essential to voice phenomena. Noah suggested I might be enclosed in a light-tight cabinet while leaving the hall in full illumination. The microphone would be outside the cabinet which would have a heavy curtain hung in front of it and secured at the sides. It was decided to construct an experimental cabinet on these lines for me although privately I wondered if I would be able to stand the heat and airlessness of a cabinet such as they so gaily planned, for periods which could be as long as an hour or more.

But before there was time to construct the cabinet for the experiments which Noah had in mind, Miss Tucker and her husband Dr Louis Young called on me at Edith's house with a proposition. They told us they proposed to invest some surplus funds in property and they suggested that if they bought a suitable house nearer London than St Albans we could rent it from them at exactly the same rent as Edith was paying for her council house. This seemed a quixotic notion to me but Miss Tucker disagreed. She said her motives were largely selfish because it was not convenient for her to trail down to St Albans every time she and her husband wanted to sit with me. She added that sooner or later I would in any case have to move nearer to London as my work became more widely known so why not make the move now on terms which would suit not only her convenience but her pocket. I queried whether it would suit her pocket and she said she had a good instinct for money and she felt strongly a purchase in the Hendon area would eventually appreciate greatly in value. I kept quiet during the discussion about capital, interest, mortgage and profit which followed because though I flattered myself I could manage my own small income capably I was completely lost when it came to any higher level of finance. Eventually Edith and Miss Tucker came to an agreement and I gathered we would rent a house from Miss Tucker in the Hendon district when we had found a suitable property. It was decided we would all go in Miss Tucker's car one day in the following week to look for it.

On the appointed day we set out in the car with a list of houses to view in the Hendon area. We drove round each house on the list looking over one or two, but in some cases we did not even trouble to go inside. Finally we arrived at 31 Sydney Grove, which was the last house on the list. Sydney Grove was a quiet cul-de-sac and I liked the look of No. 31 the moment I saw it. A dear old couple, a real Darby and Joan, owned the house and I felt they had lived in it and loved it for a long time, the very air in the house breathed happiness and serenity. Without hesitation all of us agreed this was where we would live and within a few weeks it was ours.

The removers' van stopped outside our council house and soon all our furniture and possessions were stowed inside. In the car which Miss Tucker had sent to collect us we trailed behind the van to our new home, Edith, Owen and myself, and Rags the mongrel dog we all loved. Rags seemed calmer and more confident in the future than any of us. I wondered what was in store for all of us and mourned my mission in Watford. I had done such satisfying work there. Then Edith murmured, 'It's all right, dear,' and suddenly it was.

Seven

OUR new home in Hendon soon became such a centre of psychic and spiritual activity that I and members of my regular circle decided to form an association with the object of providing evidence of the continuity of life after physical death by the demonstration of psychic gifts. A constitution was drawn up and a committee was elected to conduct its affairs and we named it the Temple of Light.

I continued to work with the Link Organisation and at regular intervals I gave public demonstrations of the direct voice in some of the biggest halls in London in front of audiences of up to two thousand people. They came to these demonstrations from all over the country. Coach-loads of people would book whole blocks of seats and some remarkable evidence was given in spite of the fact that it was impossible completely to darken these large halls and the light which streamed in made contact with the other side more difficult. Nevertheless the voices came and addressed friends and relatives in the audience to give their proof of continuing existence and many thousands were given conviction and their lives changed for the better.

My postbag was enormous and the Society was forced to employ a full-time secretary to answer the hundreds of letters which came from all over the world. The job was no sinecure, the hours were long, the work unending and the pay comparatively small but we were lucky enough to find the perfect treasure in Bunny Parsons, a former continuity girl at Elstree Studios.

Dr Louis Young and his wife were frequent visitors to us at Sydney Grove and because of Dr Young's scientific curiosity and his interest in psychical research I submitted to many tests he devised to establish the objectivity of the voices and the genuineness of my mediumship. Dr Young had sat with many mediums both in this country and in the States and he had read widely in the literature of psychical research and so his knowledge of the subject was comprehensive. Because of his work with Edison devising tricks and illusions for Maskelyne and Devant he was well aware of the tricks fraudulent mediums could contrive and he had unmasked not a few of these in his researches in America. He was the friend and supporter of those mediums he found to be genuine, but he had nothing but contempt for the frauds who batten on the bereaved and bring disgrace and shame on Spiritualism.

The tests he conducted with me made fraud impossible yet I was never made uncomfortable or subjected to mental strain. One simple but effective test he devised was carried out successfully in our seance room during one of the regular sittings we held at the Temple of Light. When I had been securely roped to my chair and just before the light was turned off Dr Young put into a measured glass enough coloured water for me to hold in my mouth for the duration of the seance. The lights were then turned out and after a short wait Mickey, my Cockney boy control, was heard speaking in his usual clear and distinctive voice. For twenty minutes thereafter various voices spoke until the seance ended and the light was turned on again, whereupon, I returned my mouthful of coloured water into the measured glass and all present saw the amount was only fractionally less than it originally was. Anyone who cares to try this test for himself will find how impossible it is to speak with his mouth filled with water and how difficult not to swallow at least a small amount of it during a period of twenty minutes.

About this time materialised forms were beginning to manifest in our regular circle through my mediumship, and Dr Young suggested we should sit by the light of a dim red bulb in order that the members of the circle could see me and the materialisations at the same time. When this was done, Dr Young and the circle members were satisfied that the apparitions were distinct and separate from my body. These materialisations were quite firm and solid and they could be felt as well as seen. They would move round the circle and sometimes they would speak to the members. I was not entranced during these manifestations and I was aware of an icy clammy coldness enveloping me while the forms built up and there was a faint odour about them which I found disagreeable. This rare type of phenomenon ceased after a while and we were told by the Guides of the circle that they had been experimenting with my physical power only to find that the materialisations detracted from the strength of the voices, and they considered it better to concentrate on my voice mediumship in order to reach many hundreds of people through the meetings in the big halls. I was glad when the materialisations stopped because apart from the unpleasant sensations during the seances I was absolutely exhausted and very nervy and irritable when they were over.

I was young, in my mid-twenties and at the peak of physical fitness, and most of my seances were highly successful, but I also had failures. Sometimes I and my sitters would wait in the darkness of the seance room for an hour and nothing at all would happen. This was very disappointing for those sitters who had travelled a great distance to sit with me as many of them did. Fortunately, most of those who sat with me were sufficiently versed in psychic science to appreciate that phenomena cannot be summoned at will and there is no question of any medium being able to 'call up the dead' as ignorant critics so often allege we do. Indeed the facts are quite otherwise. Often a sitter will come to me with the one person they long to contact strongly in mind yet that person will not manifest at all though they may obtain excellent proof of the survival of someone else in whom they have no great interest. I have never had any means of knowing in advance whether a seance will be a good one or not. If I am indisposed or over-tired, common sense tells me the chances of a good sitting will be minimal and so I do not sit in these circumstances. On the other hand there have been occasions when I have felt well and in buoyant spirits and a sitting has been a total blank. I have learned from experience that the mental attitude of the sitter is of great importance to results. A hostile approach or a selfish and demanding one can inhibit the phenomena, but honest scepticism is no barrier. A genuine medium welcomes research by those who may be unconvinced of the truth of survival provided the researcher approaches him or her in an honest and open-minded fashion, realising that mediumship is by its very nature unpredictable and that great patience is required by medium and researcher alike.

Among the many well-known people who sat with me often at the Hendon house was Shaw Desmond, the Irish novelist and playwright who was also the author of several books on psychical research. On his first visit to me he came anony-mously with a woman friend whose name he also preferred not to give. I had not the faintest idea of the identity of either of them when we sat down in the seance room and I turned out the light, but in a very few minutes Mickey announced that he was bringing Jan to speak to his father. From the boyishness of Jan's voice it was clear he must have passed to the other side of life when he was very young. The living father and the discarnate son had a long talk of a kind which any father and son might enjoy until Jan said good-bye. When he had gone I was surprised to hear the now familiar voice of Rudolph Valentino address the unknown lady. From what they said to each other it was clear they had known one another during his lifetime. Eventually the lady asked him if he could remember where they had last met and Valentino

One of a series of stringent test seances, with members of the Society for Psychical Research, at which infra-red telescopes and throat microphones were used

Another test seance on the premises of the Society for Psychical Research with the Rev. Drayton Thomas and researchers from the Society

Leslie – a recent portrait (Bram Rogers)

replied by naming a restaurant in New York where they had dined and danced.

After the sitting Shaw Desmond introduced himself and his companion who turned out to be the beautiful and talented former Gaiety Girl, Ruby Miller. She told me she had often dined with Valentino in New York but the occasion in the restaurant he had named was the last time they met before his untimely death. She added that whenever they were out together they spent most of their time talking about psychic matters in which both were passionately interested and they would often have a quiet laugh to think how disappointed the gossip-writers would be if they could only hear them.

Shaw Desmond became a regular sitter and sometimes he would be on the platform when I gave public demonstrations of my mediumship in the big London halls. He would give a short talk on my direct voice gift in which he vouched for its genuineness and recount some of his own experiences at my seances.

At one big meeting in the Aeolian Hall when he was on the platform and the spirit voices were addressing their friends in the audience, giving proofs of their identity, a religious bigot shouted from the balcony, 'God is not in this,' and kept on shouting that the seance must be stopped 'in the name of Jesus Christ!' The audience started to sing and stewards escorted the interrupter, a woman, out of the hall and the demonstration was resumed. When it was over Shaw Desmond addressed the audience and said one of the missions of the Spiritualist movement must be to convert the Christian churches back to Christianity which, in the days when its Founder walked the earth, was made manifest by the demonstration of those spiritual gifts which the Churches of today try to suppress.

At this period I was sitting regularly for a group of brave clergymen who called themselves The Confraternity. These men had become convinced of the reality of communication between this world and the next by sitting with various reputable mediums over a period of years, and it was their aim to bring Spiritualism within the framework of the Christian Church as part of the act of worship. When they had achieved this they envisaged the mediums whose gifts made such communion possible would be guarded against the misuse of their gifts and their material needs provided for by the Church in the same way as those of the clergy are met.

One might have imagined the hierarchy of the Church would welcome the idea of offering proof of its own doctrine of life everlasting within its own doors but such was far from being the case and the pioneers of The Confraternity faced considerable hostility both by way of reprimands from their superiors and militant reaction from their own brethren.

The Rev. Arthur Sharp of St Stephen's Church, Hampstead, was one of the members of this band of pioneers who sat with me often, and in fact eventually he became our president at the Temple of Light.

I remember a group arranged by the Rev. Charles Drayton Thomas who was one of the leading members of The Confraternity. Dray, as we called him, had chosen this group with care, employing spiritual need as the yardstick of entry, and I was the medium he chose to sit with them.

Before Dray put out the light in the seance room I let my eyes travel over the faces of his group. I know poverty so well I could tell these people were very poor and I prayed I might be used to bring them comfort and whatever help each individual might need.

Once the lights were out Mickey spoke almost at once and brought various friends and relations to prove their continued existence. The sitting was nearing its end when a man's voice called for 'Annie Blyth'. A woman in the group admitted to being Annie Blyth and inquired somewhat suspiciously, 'Who are you, anyway?' 'I am Fred Blythe,' answered the spirit. 'I wasn't good to you when I was on earth, Annie, and I've come to say how sorry I am and to ask your forgiveness.'

'Well,' said Annie, with considerable fire, 'you can just b—
off again. I had my fill of you when you were here, a right
rotten husband you were. Go on! B— off I tell you!'

The voice of the luckless Fred faded out in confusion and
Mickey came back to beg the recalcitrant Annie to forgive her
husband who truly repented of his ill behaviour on earth.
Though he pleaded with her, telling her of Fred's agonies of
remorse and his longing for one small word of forgiveness,
Annie refused to budge and the seance was closed.

One day Father Sharp brought an elderly lady to one of
the group seances without telling me who she was or anything
about her, which was invariably his practice. After we had
been sitting for a few minutes Mickey came through to say
there was a man called Alex present who wanted to speak to
'the new lady', and soon a strong male voice called out 'Julia!
Julia!' The new lady responded and the man continued,
'This is Alex, your father, I am here with Emily, your mother.
We have come together to speak to you. We had our differ-
ences when we were on your side of life, mostly my fault, but
now we understand each other better. I wish I had done
differently on earth but here is Mother to speak to you.' A
cultured feminine voice then spoke. 'Hello, Julia darling, it's
Mother, I've been watching over you all these years. I've
brought Fred and Dennis and I hope they'll be able to speak
to you in a moment.' When this lady had faded out, a man
announced himself as Fred and from the conversation between him and the new lady I realised he was Fred Terry, the
famous actor-manager, and the new lady was his wife. This
told me she was Julia Neilson Terry, the well known and
charming actress. When Fred Terry had said good-bye, Dennis Neilson Terry spoke and sent his love to his sister and to
his two daughters, Hazel and Monica. He asked his mother to
come again to talk to him and to try and bring Phyllis. Just
before the sitting closed Fred Terry returned to say his sister
Nell wanted to say a few words. Ellen Terry then spoke in the
soft and beautiful diction we later learned to know well in

our groups when she became one of our regular and very welcome communicators. Even now she will often come to speak to members of the theatrical profession when they sit with me.

One afternoon I was waiting for two ladies to turn up for an appointment which had been made by telephone in the names of Mrs Brown and Miss Smith. I was thinking somewhat wryly they might have shown a little more imagination in their choice of pseudonyms; the blatancy of these made the ladies' suspicions of me very obvious. I had learned the hard way to be philosophical about attitudes people adopted towards me. There were those who were unflatteringly surprised to find I was an ordinary man, neither weird nor spooky. Others made it abundantly clear, their only purpose in sitting with me was to find out what trick I employed to produce the voices. Others again would try to put me on a pedestal, prepared to worship. At first it had hurt me deeply to be suspected of charlatanry, I was so filled with the wonder of my own gift, so urgent with the desire to help and comfort all who needed me, it felt like a blow in the face when I sensed suspicion of disbelief. But now I was serenely confident in my mediumship in those who guide and help me from the other side of life and no one could hurt or discomfort me. When the ladies arrived I greeted them pleasantly and showed them into the seance room. They were both in their late middle age and dressed smartly but most discreetly.

After a short wait Mickey gave them his usual cheerful greeting and then he gave place to a man who announced himself as Alec. One of the ladies reponded by asking for his surname and the entity said he was Alec Holden. An animated conversation took place between Alec and the lady who had responded to him. It seemed she was Alec Holden's widow and that she and the friend with her occupied some position of great trust, but what it was was not made clear. Before Alec Holden said good-bye he said that someone who in life had been an important personage was going to speak to them. As soon as Alec's voice faded, the voice of an elderly man was heard trying to make himself understood and obviously having difficulty in doing so. After a while his voice became stronger and clearer and whoever it was said how nice it was to speak to the ladies again. At this point I was surprised to hear my sitters pushing back their chairs and scuffling with their feet. I simply could not imagine what they were doing. I was even more flummoxed when in tones of the deepest respect they said in unison, 'Your Majesty!' and the voice replied, 'Yes, I am George, who was known on earth as King George the Fifth.' Some talk ensued between this entity and my sitters. He sent his love to May and Louise and his blessings to his sons before his voice faded.

Afterwards Mrs Holden and her friend made themselves known to me and revealed they had been attached to the Royal Household for many years and they had recognised the voice of the late King as soon as he managed to enunciate clearly. They claimed the voice was so unmistakably the late King's that both of them had automatically risen from their chairs and curtseyed as soon as they heard it. They asked if they might come again and bring a friend whose name they would prefer not to tell me. I agreed to give them another booking on these terms.

When they came the next time they brought with them a tall, very dignified man who anxiously asked me if Mrs Holden had impressed on me his desire to remain anonymous. I reassured him, but I had to warn him that often when sitters take steps to remain unknown to me my guide Mickey has greeted them by name as soon as he comes through.

However, it was not Mickey who blew the gaff on this occasion but a woman from the other side of life who called out 'James! How are you, James? I am, or rather was Countess Camperdown.' This voice faded and was followed by a man speaking with a broad Scots accent. He announced himself as John Brown and told us he had been the trusted servant of Queen Victoria and had also acted as the medium for her communication with her beloved husband Prince Albert during her widowhood. He went on to say he was going to help Lady Camperdown to speak again because she had been a friend of his own Madam's and James had served her as faithfully as he himself had served Queen Victoria. The lady's voice returned and was heard to ask James if he remembered the old days at Weston and the house in Hill Street. After some further talk between them the lady's voice faded and the seance ended.

When the light was turned on, the man, overwhelmed by what he had heard, threw anonymity to the wind and introduced himself as John James. He told me he had been a footman in the service of Countess Camperdown many years before, when he was a young man. He had served her both at her country estate, Weston in Warwickshire, and at her town house in Hill Street, Mayfair. Since Lady Camperdown's death he had been in service in various houses of those the world calls great and at that time he was and had been for many years house steward to H.R.H. Princess Louise at Kensington Palace.

Princess Louise was Queen Victoria's fourth daughter and sixth child and she was then almost ninety years of age. Mr James was so impressed with the evidence he had been given he asked if he could book a regular sitting with me and then and there I arranged a monthly appointment for him. When the stately Mr James had thus set the seal of his approval on me Mrs Holden confided in me that she had been for a number of years an honorary lady-in-waiting to the Princess Louise.

John James was born in a mountain village in Wales in 1872 and he was already in his sixties when we met. All his life had been spent in the service of others more privileged than himself, but there was none of the resentment of the truly servile in this man. He had true dignity and great integrity. He was a man who knew exactly who he was. He expected high standards of personal conduct from those he served and if they proved unworthy of his respect he ceased to serve them. To those who had earned them he gave all his loyalty and all his devotion not just for the wages or the perquisites which might come his way but simply because he was a man who was incapable of giving less than his best.

James became very important in my life because through him I met so many interesting people on both sides of life. I used eagerly to look forward to his sittings, wondering which of the once high and mighty would come to talk with him. Queen Victoria came often and she would send loving messages to her daughter Louise and to various other members of the Family. Invariably, in her messages to Princess Louise, she would give some small personal detail or recall some memory of the Princess's childhood so that when James gave her the message she would know it was truly her mother who had spoken.

On one occasion Queen Victoria thanked James for the healing he had given to her daughter and later I learned that he was a natural spiritual healer and he had many times been able to relieve the acute pain of the arthritis from which Princess Louise suffered.

At one of James' sittings a man came through and gave his name as John Sutherland. He sent his dearest love to Louise and asked James to tell her he had their dog Tina with him. After the sitting I learned that John Sutherland had been the Marquis of Lorne, later the Duke of Argyll, whom the princess married in 1871 in St George's Chapel, Windsor, when Queen Victoria herself gave her daughter away. The occasion was perhaps only slightly marred by the atrocious pun perpetrated by Dean Alford who referred to the bride as 'the maiden all for Lorne'. It was a marriage of true lovers and they were ideally happy until the Duke's death in 1914. The message he sent her by James meant a great deal to her. Tina had been a pet the princess and her husband had loved dearly many years before and they had been deeply grieved when she was run over and killed by a motor-car. According to James they had been so upset by Tina's death that the Duke had composed an epitaph in verse which they had had engraved on a headstone to mark her grave.

James relied on me implicitly not to discuss his seances with anyone nor ever to divulge to a soul that he received and passed on messages to various members of the royal family. The family were in duty bound to uphold the religion of the State which did not regard Spiritualism with any great favour and it could have proved an embarrassment to them if these seances had become public knowledge. Until now no word of them has ever passed my lips nor been committed to paper, but now all those intimately concerned have passed to life's other side and the climate of opinion is so vastly different from that of thirty years ago I feel free to tell this story for the first time.

'You must find a tailor and get a suit made, Leslie,' said Edith at breakfast one morning. 'You simply can't be seen on a public platform again in that frightful old reach-me-down.'

I viewed her over the marmalade with alarm. 'I paid fifty bob for that suit. There's years of wear in it yet. Besides, I've never had a suit made for me in my entire life. I'm not made of money.'

'When you walked on to the platform at the Wigmore Hall last night, in front of all those people, with trousers like a pair of concertinas and that sagging jacket, Owen and I decided it was time you had a decent suit made for you.'

I looked across the table at Owen, now a handsome lad of eighteen. He grinned at me. 'There were all the nobs on the platform in their Savile Row gents' bespoke and the star of the show walks on in his cheap old suit. It won't do, old chap.'

Mentally I reviewed my finances. Certainly I was better off than I had ever been before, people from all over the country were queuing up to sit with me and I was given a percentage of the takings at the meetings in the big halls which were always packed to the doors, but my expenses were heavy and it was not my practice to charge more for my sittings than even the poorest could afford. Also the old fear of being out of work still gnawed at my vitals and I tried to save as much as I could against that evil day. I shook my head. 'I can't afford it,' I said.

'I'll chip in a few quid,' said Owen cheerfully. Sheer human decency can always bring the tears to my eyes and I had to swallow very hard. When Owen had left school a couple of years before, a friend of mine had kindly found him a place as a junior with one of the camera crews at the studios in Boreham Wood. Owen loved the work and he hoped one day to become a star lighting cameraman like Günther Krampf or Jimmy Harvey, brother of the enchanting Lilian, the radiant star of *Congress Dances*. Owen earned very little but he contributed to the household budget and I knew he was secretly saving every penny he could spare to buy the motor-bike he so badly wanted. Yet here he was offering me his savings to buy a suit. 'Don't be silly,' I said gruffly, 'of course I can find the money for a suit if your mother thinks I need one.' As soon as I said it I felt a familiar chill of fear. 'Don't worry, dear,' Edith said, 'I'll find a tailor who won't rook you and I can easily cut down on the housekeeping.' She could always make the sun come out again.

It seems unbelievable now, but since the move to Hendon I had been so isolated in the ivory tower of my work, so wrapped in a cocoon of domestic content I was only half aware of the man Hitler and the evil which was creeping over the face of Germany.

I was measured for my suit in a room over a sweetshop in Golders Green where for a few pounds Nathan Hirsch worked with the dedicated skill of a master craftsman. With the help of the dictionary with which he was trying to learn the language of the country where he must remake his life, Mr Hirsch told me what was happening to his people in Germany. By the time he had finished my suit Hitler's field-grey automata were marching into Austria. England consoled herself with eye-witness accounts in the newspapers which told of tanks made of cardboard, guns without bullets, planes unable to leave the ground, and ill-clad teenage soldiers. We breathed again, Hitler was not ready, there would be no war.

One day during the summer which followed the rape of Austria John James was taking his leave after one of his regular sittings when he said casually, 'Would it be convenient for you to call at Kensington Palace on Thursday next at three o'clock?' I gaped at him stupidly. He explained the Princess Louise wanted to meet me and since she was shortly leaving London, the following Thursday would suit her admirably. My appointment book was crammed but I had a vague idea that royal invitations were tantamount to commands and visions of a dungeon in the Tower floated through my confused mind. I would just have to re-arrange my appointments somehow. I said Thursday would suit me fine.

Spruce in Mr Hirsch's navy pin-stripe, the cut of which I thought even a princess of the blood must approve, I emerged from the underground station at Hyde Park Corner on the big day to find that in my nervous anxiety to be punctual I had left myself an hour for the fifteen-minute bus journey to Kensington. I decided to stroll through the Park to the Palace.

It was a glorious afternoon and halfway to my destination I sat down on a bench to feast on a scarlet blaze of geraniums and to consider how unlikely and how absurd it was that I should be on my way to call on a royal princess in her palace. I wondered if her flunkeys would look down their noses at me. I had never met a flunkey but I had a feeling they would be snotty and supercilious persons. I consoled myself with the thought of Mr Hirsch's impeccable tailoring and dismissed them. A new thought disturbed me. Did one kiss the hand of a princess on being presented and if so how was it done? I had a sudden flash of an actor in some film I had seen planting a kiss on a lady's palm and nibbling halfway up her arm and rejected this technique as inappropriate. Unhappily certain that if there was any pitfall of etiquette into which I might flounder, I would be bound to do so, I proceeded on my way.

In the event John James met me at the entrance of the palace and as he conducted me to what he called the small drawing-room he gave me a few hints as to how to conduct myself towards my royal hostess.

Compared to 31 Sydney Grove the small drawing-room did not look all that small to me. H.R.H. Princess Louise was sitting very upright on a chair with a high carved back when James ushered me into the room and the hand-kissing problem was settled right away when she held out her hand in a friendly way like any other hostess might do. When I had lightly touched hands with the Princess she waved me to a comfortable chair and invited James also to be seated. I took stock of my surroundings and absurdly enough I was reminded of the parlour of which my grandmother was so proud. This room was infinitely more rich and splendid but the heavy furniture, the velvet curtains at the windows, the wealth of statuary and bric-à-brac and the pictures crowding the walls had the same fusty flavour of the room which was Gran's pride and joy. There was even a smell of wax polish. The fact was of course that both rooms reflected the taste of a bygone age and both belonged to elderly women to whom the past was more vivid than the present.

The Princess started the conversational ball rolling by asking if I had noticed the statue of Queen Victoria in her coronation robes outside the palace. She told me she had herself designed and executed it from a single piece of Carrara marble to mark the fiftieth year of the reign. Princess Louise, clearly, had been devoted to Queen Victoria to whom she referred rather touchingly as 'Mamma'.

The ice thus broken we talked easily together for an hour or more about my work and about the evidence in the messages which James had conveyed to her from her mother and her husband. I remember her saying she no longer had the slightest fear of death and she looked on it as a kind of emigration to a new country where she would rejoin those she had loved who had travelled there before her. She mentioned the difficulties she had sometimes encountered because of her royal birth and told me how she would often tell those who were uncomfortable or inhibited in her presence that she could not help being a queen's daughter and they must try not to mind it. She talked most happily about her girlhood at Windsor Castle and of the period she and her husband had spent in Canada while he was Governor-General there. She was very proud of the fact that the Canadians had named their new province Alberta because it was one of her christian names.

Although the Princess gave no outward sign of it I got a strong impression after a while that she was suffering intense pain and so when she suggested ringing for tea I glanced questioningly at James. He shook his head slightly and I excused myself and took my leave of a very gracious and gentle lady.

When I got off the bus at Hyde Park Corner to get the Tube to Hendon my heart sank to see the news bills outside the Underground Station. Hitler was at it again. This time he was demanding the Sudetenland from the Czechs.

In the train I thought back to my childhood in the aftermath of that war which was to end all war. I saw again the men who came back crippled, shell-shocked, the tissues of their lungs rotted by poison gas, waiting, patient and hopeless in the long queues for the dole, and I prayed the senseless slaughter and squalor of war would not come again.

During this summer of mounting tension and anxiety over the Czech crisis my work continued, but there were more failures than usual and those who guide me from the other side told us the atmosphere surrounding the earth was so filled with fear and thoughts of war that it was hard for those who live in the light to penetrate what appeared to them as a thick fog.

There were successful seances too, of course, and recently I received a letter dated 4 June 1970 from Mr William A. Pritchard of 85 Bishopston Road, Swansea, to remind me of one of them. I do not think I can do better than quote an extract from it here:

My one and only sitting with you took place over 30 years ago in the summer of 1938. My mother was with me, she was in this country on holiday from Rhodesia where she and my father were then living. We made our booking by phone and no names were either requested or given. There were about eight sitters and the voices came quite independently of any trumpet and all sitters had contact with someone during the evening. A voice addressed me:

VOICE: Hello, I thought I would come and make myself known.
W.A.P.: Very nice. But who are you?
VOICE: Dick.
W.A.P.: And where did we know each other?
VOICE: We were in the Air Force together in South Africa.
W.A.P.: How did you manage to get to where you are?
VOICE: Well, you know how it was ... I was on my motor-bike and I hit a brick wall and next thing I knew I was here ...

My memory went back some 12 years to the very short time I had spent in the South African Air Force. Among the apprentices was a youngster known to everyone as 'Bonzo'. He was a pleasant but very slow-witted boy with a curious affliction in that his hands were sort of 'over-co-ordinated'. Whatever he did with one hand, the other hand automatically did the same thing unless Bonzo made a definite effort of will to stop it. The story of Bonzo's passing had been sent to me shortly after my return to England in 1929. It appears he had acquired a motor-bike and was out for a spin and travelling up the stem of a 'T' junction. He put out his right arm to indicate intention, his left arm went out in sympathy and Bonzo went straight into a brick wall ahead of him. The year after my sitting with you, in 1939, I went back to South Africa and when in Pretoria I took a trip up to Roberts Heights, the headquarters of the South African Air Force. In the Orderly Room were a couple of sergeants who remembered me and also remembered Bonzo, but even they did not know his real name. We looked up the records and discovered it was Richard Lundin.

Whenever I am asked what I consider to be the most evidential sentence I have received at a seance, I quote the ten words 'We were in the Air Force together in South Africa' because no one in that room in your house had any idea my mother and I had any connection with South Africa, let alone the Air Force.

Eight

FOR months after war broke out Britain existed in the uneasy calm of the phony war. It was a kind of no-man's-land in time when we accustomed ourselves to the blackout and rationing and the infringements of personal liberty. So apparently normal was the surface of life that many began to hope the half-hearted hostilities would peter out altogether in a negotiated peace which they thought would be a victory for civilisation. Meanwhile, factories, shipyards and arsenals worked full blast preparing for the real war to come.

My first public direct voice seance in wartime was held in the Rochester Square Temple in north London. The Temple had a glass roof which had been coated with black paint to conform with the blackout regulations. I cannot tell how effective this may have been at night as seen from the air but it certainly did not prevent daylight from flooding the hall. However, I took my place in a hastily improvised cabinet on the platform and hoped for the best. To quote from a contemporary report of this meeting by A. W. Austen: 'in spite of the adverse conditions voices were heard all over the hall although no microphones were used'.

Towards the end of this meeting as I sat in my dark airless cabinet wondering how long I could last before I passed out from the heat and nervous exhaustion I heard a woman's voice speaking so near my cabinet she seemed almost to be addressing herself personally to me.

'I am Edith Cavell,' said the voice. 'I came to this side of life because I felt patriotism was not enough. Although I admire the man and the woman who is patriotic, at the same time we must realise there is a greater thing than that. You must love your brother whether he be an enemy or not. Try to love and forgive, not to hate.'

The voice faded but its message remained to help me to resolve a problem which had been giving me much anxious thought ever since the outbreak of war.

I had so often listened to the voices from beyond the grave of men and women who had been cut off in the prime of their lives by sudden death. They had spoken of their confusion and distress and how they had to cling to the familiar earth because it was all they had ever known. I had heard their reproaches. 'Why didn't I know? Why didn't someone tell me?' I was a patriot and my country was at war for a cause I believed to be just. But when this dreamlike half-war turned into the real thing the killing would begin in earnest and like other young fit men I would be called to join the Services. Yet after all I had heard from the other side of life about the soul's bewilderment when it is thrust suddenly out of its physical body into the next plane of existence. How could I be responsible for sending any human spirit into eternity unprepared? I had a quick memory of a scene which had taken place in my childhood during the unveiling of a 1914–18 war memorial. During the ceremony a group of women converged on a man who was standing watching. The women jostled and pushed and shouted at him and at last the man went away. When I asked my grandmother what the man had done wrong she told me he had been a 'conchie' during the war and these women had lost sons in the fighting. I was sorry for those women whose grief had turned to resentment against someone they thought of as a shirker, but I saw that perhaps it took a special kind of courage to swim against the tide of war. I only hoped I would find it because then and there I made up my mind that when the time came to stand up and be counted I would be a conscientious objector. I would say with Martin Luther, 'Here I stand. I can do no other.'

Some weeks later I received a letter from a member of a wealthy Spiritualist organisation in America. The writer said he had attended one of my public seances in London and had subsequently sat with me privately at my home in Hendon. He described the evidence he had been given at this sitting and said it had proved to him beyond doubt the survival of someone dear to him. Because he and his colleagues feared my mediumship might be lost to the world if I remained in England they offered me sanctuary in their country for the duration of the war. My passage would be arranged and my livelihood would be guaranteed for as long as it was advisable for me to remain in the States. It may seem illogical that I who had so firmly rejected the thought of taking up arms should feel highly indignant that anyone should imagine I would leave England at this time but that was exactly how I felt. As politely as I could I refused this well-meant offer by return of post.

Christmas came and the war was still in a state of uneasy stalemate. The three of us at Sydney Grove tried hard to pretend everything was just as it had always been. We ate the traditional food, we did the traditional things, we took very special pains over the surprises we planned for each other. Perhaps we tried too hard for there was no heart, no real joy in any of it. How could there be when we feared that just over the horizon of the coming year the storm which had been gathering so long must surely break?

On New Year's Eve, Edith produced from its hiding-place a bottle of sparkling wine to toast not only a new year but a whole new decade. On the stroke of midnight we raised our glasses and wished each other the old wish and sang Auld Lang Syne with Edith's velvet contralto giving a new meaning and a deeper emotion to the words we had sung unthinkingly so often in the past.

Early in 1940 I gave a seance which not only produced some

first-class evidence of man's survival of his bodily death but I think it was one of the most unusual sittings I have ever given and it certainly provided me with some needed light relief.

The sitter gave her name as Mrs Bowering and she appeared to be somewhere in her late sixties. We went into the seance room and sat down without any preliminary chit-chat and I turned out the light. Mickey spoke to the lady almost at once. 'There's a man here who says his name is Fred and that you are his wife, Alice.'

'Yes,' said Mrs Bowering, 'Fred is my husband. Can I talk to him, please?' Shortly, a man's voice spoke and he and Mrs Bowering had an intimate and personal conversation about their past together until suddenly he said laughingly, 'Fancy you taking the trouble to have my body taken out of its grave after all these years and having it cremated! I see you are wearing the ring you buried with me on your finger at this moment! I've met Bowering over here, you know, and we like each other very much. As a matter of fact it amuses both of us that you should have my ashes in one urn on the mantelpiece and his ashes in another.'

Mrs Bowering then inquired if Mr Bowering could speak to her and soon the voice of another man greeted her. 'You know, Alice,' he said, 'even though you've put Fred's urn and mine on the mantelpiece we are not really there. We are here and we come often together to try to help you as well as we may but these ashes really have nothing to do with us any more.' To my astonishment Mrs Bowering then told both her late husbands she had met a man called Wilson and she was seriously considering marriage with him. She wanted to know if either of them would object to this. Both Fred and Mr Bowering said they had no objection at all and the only thing they wanted was the happiness of Alice.

I found this story of the ashes of two husbands in urns on the same mantelpiece so hard to swallow that when the light was turned on again I asked the lady if it was true. She said it most certainly was true and told me what great trouble she had had getting permission to exhume Fred in order to have him cremated. It seemed that in the days she had buried Fred cremation had not been a usual method of disposal and so she had buried him in the conventional way. But things had changed when Mr Bowering's time had come and so he had been cremated, and the urn containing his ashes adorned her mantelpiece. After a while she had begun to feel Fred might feel slighted all alone in the cemetery and so she had started her campaign to have him exhumed to be cremated and placed alongside Mr Bowering. She had finally achieved this and now she had both husbands to hand as it were, she felt much happier. She also confirmed that a ring she was wearing had lain in the grave on Fred's finger for many years. She was glad neither husband objected to a third marriage because she found life on her own very lonely.

I did not see this lady for a couple of years after this sitting and so I assumed she had married again and was once more living happily in double harness. As it turned out I was wrong. Long afterwards she came to sit with me in her new role as Mrs Wilson and her first two husbands came again to speak to her. She spent her entire sitting berating both of them for not warning her Wilson was not only 'a man of dirty habits' but he had no money and she was forced to support him. Her late husbands expressed regret that matters had turned out badly but they pointed out the decision to marry Wilson had been her own and she must take responsibility for it. However, it was the freely expressed view of Mrs Wilson that they ought to have known in advance how her third husband would turn out and given her fair warning. Mrs Wilson sat with me regularly until her death at the age of eighty. She lived apart from Mr Wilson for many years and he died before she did. I sometimes wonder even now which husband has the pleasure of her company on the other side and how Mr Wilson fits into the picture.

Princess Louise had died early in December 1939 and John James had not been able to come to me for his regular sittings because he was very fully occupied in clearing the contents of the Princess's apartments of nearly a hundred rooms under the direction of the then Duke of Kent to whom the contents of the Palace had been left in her will. However, in late March 1940 Mr James telephoned for a sitting and I was happy to give one to him.

I think both James and I felt sad sitting together for the first time since the passing of the gentle princess. But if we did, it was not for long because Princess Louise herself spoke to us and told us how happy she was to be free of pain and the infirmities of old age and to be reunited with those she loved. She thanked James for doing what she had asked about the wedding veil and her rings. After the sitting, James told me the Princess was referring to the fact that she had asked to be covered in death with her wedding veil and for her engagement and wedding rings to be put in the casket with her ashes. Before he left that day James showed me with great pride a pair of monogrammed cuff-links which the Duke of Kent had given him for his help in clearing up the apartments in Kensington Palace.

In April of that year Germany invaded Norway and the war began in earnest. While the Allies were attempting to land forces in Norway to help the Norwegians and all Britain waited breathlessly from one news bulletin to the next Owen came home one evening and told his mother and me he had volunteered for the Royal Air Force and had been passed medically fit for air crew. 'When do you have to go?' asked Edith, trying hard to sound matter of fact. 'When they are in trouble, they'll send for Mundin,' quipped Owen, 'I'm to stay put until then.' Even this respite comforted Edith, the evil day was not yet. When Owen lightly inquired what branch of the Forces I proposed to favour with my presence I told him I intended to register as a conscientious objector when my call-up came. I watched for the contempt I dreaded to see in this boy I loved as a brother. He quirked his eyebrow in a way which was specially his, 'Good for you,' he said lightly. 'I simply don't have that particular kind of courage.'

In May and June we learned the new word blitzkrieg as the Nazi hammer-blows crushed Holland, Belgium and France and forced the British out of Europe at Dunkirk where, by what seemed a miracle at the time, most of our troops were brought home to fight again another day.

They were dangerous days, highly charged with emotion, and constantly I questioned within myself whether I could really stand back and let others do the fighting. I wanted to serve, I wanted to help, I thought the war a just one if any war could be considered just, but always I came back to the fact that I could not, I would not kill.

Later that year after the Battle of Britain had been fought and won in the skies over England, Owen was posted to an airfield near Cambridge to begin his training as a pilot.

When Edith and I saw him off at the station he was gay and full of confidence. 'Relax, you two,' he joked, 'any minute now Mundin, the terror of the skies, will be on the job.' As the train started to move he leaned out of the carriage window and kissed Edith. 'I'll be back, old lady,' he said gently. 'We'll have a nice cup of tea,' I said, and I do not think I have ever in my life felt so inadequate.

At last the day came when I had to appear before a tribunal to state my case as a conscientious objector. I took the train to London and spent some time searching for the hall near Victoria Station where the court was sitting with Judge Hargreaves as president. Eventually I found the place and I was ushered into an ante-room where a number of other 'conchies' were waiting to be heard. I sat down next to a young fellow with a fair straggly beard who at once produced a slim volume from his pocket and began to read with great concentration. I took the hint and bit back the casual pleasantry I had been about to utter. When I looked round I saw that no one was talking to his neighbour, all the young men were sitting silent and withdrawn, each intent on his own thoughts, his own problem.

We were being heard alphabetically so it was not too long before the usher put his head round the door and called 'Flint, Leslie!' I followed him out of the room.

As I walked down the hall to the table where the five members of the tribunal were sitting I was surprised to see spectators in the hall. Whether they were the friends and relatives of the men being heard or merely inquisitive members of the public I do not know, but I could very gladly have done without them. I was glad to see the members of the tribunal were wearing ordinary clothes, I had had some confused idea they would be garbed in awe-inspiring robes and wigs. There was even a woman among them with a reassuringly frivolous hat on her carefully waved hair. As it turned out the lady with the daisies on her bonnet was the toughest nut of all.

I stood in front of the five keepers of my conscience and straightened my shoulders, determined not to look hangdog or ashamed. Answering leading questions, I agreed I was Leslie Flint, thirty years of age and as far as I knew, fit and healthy. I also affirmed that on grounds of conscience I was unable and unwilling to serve in the armed forces in the present state of emergency.

'Kindly tell the tribunal whether your scruples are of a political or a religious nature, Flint.' Thus the President opening the bowling. I said I absolutely refused to take human life on religious grounds. An elderly man with a heavy moustache asked me what church I belonged to. 'I am the resident medium of a Christian Spiritualist church in Hendon,' I said. The elderly man blew through his moustache, reminding me of a petulant walrus. 'Not a recognised denomination of the Christian church,' he said in triumph. The President thought it would meet the case if I were described as a Christian pacifist. The Walrus whispered in the ear of the man next to him so loudly I heard, 'The fellow's a crank of some kind.'

A red-faced man inquired if I thought Christ was a pacifist. I said His teaching was filled with ideas of brotherly love and peace between men, and quoted the words He spoke about turning the other cheek. The red-faced man asked me what good I thought it would do to turn the other cheek to Hitler. I agreed it might be disastrous but added that this fact did not alter my determination not to kill. The hat with the daisies now turned in my direction. 'If you saw a Nazi storm-trooper trying to rape a woman you loved would you just stand back and do nothing?' she rapped out. Oh, no! I thought, Oh no, not that! 'Well?' persisted the daisy bonnet. I said I would defend the woman with all my strength whether I loved her or not but I would not kill the storm-trooper. 'If you had a knife in your hand would you use it?' From the way she spoke I thought she must have been to a very posh school when she was young. I said I would use the knife to try to stop the storm-trooper raping the lady but not to kill him. The bonnet uttered a small chirp of outrage. 'A genuine pacifist would reason with him,' she said. A vivid picture of my five feet three inches sweetly reasoning with six feet of storm-trooper mad with lust intruded on my inner eye and I felt a perilous desire to laugh.

'You would knife a man, but you wouldn't put a bullet through him in battle. Is that your position, Flint?' demanded the man with the red face, returning to the fray. I looked at the faces confronting me, honest, upright members of society trying to be fair, trying to understand, but not able to hide the growing suspicion I was a coward or a shirker. I asked the President if I might explain to the members of the tribunal the Spiritualist philosophy on which was based my determination to go to prison sooner than join the armed forces. The Walrus was heard to mutter that he did not want to listen to spook claptrap, he didn't believe in it, anyway. But the President told me to go ahead and please to be brief.

With an eloquence which surprised myself I described the confusion of a soul hurled into eternity in the heat and passion of battle with no knowledge of what lies before it on the next plane of existence. I quoted to them the solemn invocation from the Litany, 'from battle and murder and from sudden death, good Lord, deliver us', which shows that the Fathers of the early Church knew more about the after life than their successors do today. When I had finished, heads were put together and there was much whispering and conferring. Finally my Lady of the Daisies lifted up her cool clipped voice. 'Are you suggesting our brave men in the services will suffer remorse in the next life because they are killing their country's enemies?' 'No, madam,' I said, 'they will not, because they do not know, as I know, the consequences to the souls of those they send into eternity. It is precisely because I have been given that knowledge through the exercise of my gift of mediumship that I must refuse the responsibility of taking human life.' 'And yet you are not unwilling indirectly to help the armed forces to kill more efficiently?' This was the calm, detached voice of the President. I said my country was engaged in a war which I considered to be a struggle of good against evil and I would play my part to my utmost short of personally taking life. There was another whispered conference and a quiet grey-faced man who had not hitherto spoken, looked up. 'How do we know you are sincere?' he said. I approached the President and held out to him an envelope in which was the letter offering me sanctuary in America and Bunny Parsons' carbon copy of my reply. 'I think these two letters will answer the gentleman's question,' I said. The President read both the American letter and the copy of my reply and passed them round for the others to see. There was more whispering and more conferring and finally the President told me I would be called into a non-combatant corps some time in the near future.

I walked to the Underground station to take the train back to Hendon. A great bomber's moon was sailing in the sky. As I reached the station the siren wailed and the city's orchestra of defence started.

On the platform the tiered bunks were already being occupied by those who slept in them night after night in comparative safety. Families were claiming pitches where they would spread rugs and pillows or were already ensconced, eating from paper bags and drinking tea from flasks. Here and all over the hidden depths of the city was the identical smell of fear and sweat and musty used-up air and the Londoners enduring with patience and humour and their small defiance, they were such good people.

Walking home from Hendon station to the concerto of guns, falling shrapnel and the shriek and crump of bombs, I worried about how to provide for Edith when I was away on war duty. I had saved over £100 which I would leave with her and she had her own small pension, but when I thought of the rent, the rates, the heat, the light and all the other bills which arrived with depressing regularity I wondered how long £100 would last? How long would the war go on? My pay as a private soldier in a non-combatant unit would be 2s a day all found, perhaps I could squeeze 10s a week to send to Edith. I must because otherwise she would try to solve her problem by working in munitions and she was not strong enough nor any longer young enough to work long hours at a factory bench.

When I reached home Edith told me Miss Tucker and her husband had called at the house while I was in London to say they proposed to forgo the rent of 31 Sydney Grove while I was on war service. My anxieties took wing and I remembered a promise given to me long before by one of those who guide and help me from life's other side. 'You will never have all you want,' he said, 'but as long as you serve faithfully you will be provided with all you need.' I remembered how often help had come from some unexpected quarter when it was most needed and reproached myself for my lack of trust.

The day came when I had to leave my home, my work and all that was dear to me. Edith came up to London to see me off at Paddington where I was to join the train for Ilfracombe. We found the train and I saw it was full of men of my own age who were all bound for Ilfracombe and the same training course as I was. Some men kindly moved up together to make a place for me in one of the crowded carriages. I stood leaning out of the window to talk to Edith until the last second. Talk does not come easily at such a time nor in such a place and all we could find to say to each other in those moments when there was so much to be said were banalaties of the order of 'don't forget to write' and 'take care of yourself'. At last the train shuddered into movement and I kissed her and watched her blink back tears and force a smile. As the train hurried away from her I hung out of the window watching her wave until I lost sight of her in the distance. As the train carried me faster and faster to a new and unknown life I felt very lonely in that crowded carriage.

Nine

Outside Ilfracombe station two sergeants cantered to and fro like bad-tempered sheepdogs herding us into the semblance of a column. In our civilian clothes, crumpled from the journey, clutching our little cases, we must have looked a sorry sight. 'What a horrible lot!' I heard one of the sergeants say. 'A regular shower!' agreed the other.

Chivvied by our sheepdogs, out of step, straggling, we were marched down the hill to our billet which turned out to be a requisitioned hotel on the sea front which, efficiently stripped of every peacetime comfort, was now a cold and desolate barracks.

When we had been fed, two new sheepdogs formed us into line outside the Quartermaster's store to be issued with our uniform. Some of the conchies had not bargained for military uniform and the thought of it was so repugnant to them they refused point blank to accept it, let alone wear it. After a certain amount of shouting and argument, military policemen carted these recusants away and they were not seen again. I do not know what became of them but it was generally assumed they would end up in a civil prison unless they changed their minds.

When I had been given the coarse, scratchy underwear, the khaki battledress, the heavy boots and the rest of the clobber which made up my kit, I was shown where to sleep and ordered to change into my new gear. My bedchamber was a large bare room lined with double-tiered bunks which looked identical with those in the London Underground. As I dumped my kit on a top bunk I observed a large young man sitting on the lower one with tears streaming down his cheeks. I felt pretty grim myself but I tried to cheer him up as best I could. Finally I managed to coax him to change into his uniform as one of the sheepdogs had ordered us to do. When we had both donned our new clothes we looked at each other and burst out laughing. His uniform was as tight as a sausage skin while mine, several sizes too big for me, hung on me with a scarecrow effect. We laughed so hard at each other that both of us forgot our miseries. My new-found friend's name was Ernie and he was a London Cockney who had been living more by his wits than by honest toil, which fact he told me with some pride, adding that he was pretty good at avoiding work or any other kind of unpleasantness. I soon found that this was no idle boast. He was more than pretty good, he was an expert.

What I hated beyond everything during my training course at Ilfracombe was the daily drill session on the front. I could do nothing correctly, I had two left feet, I was hopeless. Sergeant Jones, the old sweat who drilled us, grew scarlet in the face and his eyes bulged out of their sockets with sheer frustration as he bawled me out for my stupid mistakes. The harder I tried to do what he wanted, the more clumsy and awkward I became and the louder he bawled. To add to the misery of it, knots of civilians would gather to watch and their uninhibited laughter infuriated Sergeant Jones and humiliated me. After a while I think Sergeant Jones came to believe I actually enjoyed being the local comic turn because he stopped bawling at me, always good for a laugh from the civilians, and simply put me on a charge when I did something idiotic. The charge was usually 'dumb insolence' against which there is no defence.

Sgt Jones' change in tactics resulted in my spending so much time on jankers, peeling potatoes or doing other fatigues that I saw very little of the town while I was stationed there. Ernie was by no means a model soldier but he always managed to avoid trouble or undue exertion and he was always amply supplied with funds. Later I learned he made a useful little income selling black market stockings to the local females; but he was a good friend and he gave up many an evening to help me to peel mountains of potatoes or polish acres of floor.

Shortly before the course ended Ernie and I were strolling in the town when we spotted a cheap photographer and we decided to have our pictures taken. When we got them they were truly dreadful. I do not know which of us looked worse. I tore up mine on the spot except for one copy which I sent to Edith, hoping it would at least make her laugh.

At last the course was over and, in theory at any rate, we had been licked into some kind of military shape. We were given travel warrants and seven days leave and told to report back to a camp on the Welsh border.

On my first night at home Edith arranged a sitting of our home circle, but it had hardly begun before the siren wailed and a heavy air-raid was soon in full swing. One or two of the members of the circle wondered if we should take cover and postpone the sitting, but the suggestion had no sooner been made than Mickey came through to veto it. He told us nothing whatsoever would happen to our house and asked us to continue the seance. We did as Mickey asked, but the raid got worse and worse until the whole house rocked on its foundations as a particularly heavy bomb fell uncomfortably close. Mickey at once returned to speak to us and told us a land mine had fallen a few streets from us and many people had been killed. He went on to say that hundreds of spirit people were already at the scene of the disaster to help the victims over the border between this life and the next and to explain to them the fact of their physical death and their continuing life in the other world. Mickey is normally gay, irrepressible, quick at repartee, but that evening he talked to us very seriously and as he talked his treble boy's voice changed its timbre and became more adult, more cultured, more resonant. The subject of Mickey's discourse was the enormous effort being made by the spirit world to ensure no victim of the war, whatever his nationality, creed or state of mind, should be left to cling to the earth because of ignorance of the life to come. He told us thousands upon thousands of spirit people had made it their work to go wherever the need arose to guide newly dead in a state of bewilderment to their place in the next life.

Later that evening, while the others were drinking rationed tea and eating wartime sandwiches, I went upstairs to fetch a cardigan for one of the ladies. The cardigan was with an assortment of wraps on Edith's counterpane and as I turned over the various garments to find it I noticed on Edith's bedside table the appalling photograph I had sent to her from Ilfracombe as a joke. Now it was in a silver frame. The thought that Edith cherished this dreadful picture touched me deeply. I made up my mind to try again to persuade her to marry me. As we washed up in the kitchen after our guests had gone, I begged her to be my wife. She produced all the old arguments I had heard so often before. I put my hand over her lips to stop her. 'It's you I want to marry,' I told her, 'no one else will do.' Two days later we were married at the local registry office and the first thing we did after the laconic little ceremony was to send Owen a telegram with the news. His reply, by return, read: 'Dearest idiots, news long overdue, so glad, Owen.' What remained of my leave we spent happily together at home.

Very few of the men I had trained with had been posted to my new camp but I was glad to find Ernie there when I arrived. Our work was laying a new railway track and from eight in the morning until nightfall we carried and laid the heavy sleepers. It was hard, tough work, but once my unaccustomed muscles were limbered up I rather enjoyed working in the fresh air and daylight as a change from years of sitting passively in a darkened room to earn my living. Also, praise be! there was no time for drill sessions in this busy workers' camp.

As far as Ernie was concerned, hard labour under the eye of a sergeant alert to pounce on slackers was an outrage. 'It's a bloomin' liberty!' he would complain angrily, 'I'm a bloke wot sees jobs get done! I don't do 'em meself! I got brains, see! They gotta nerve!' Ernie was never one to suffer passively and he set his undoubted talent to work to achieve a transfer to some less obnoxious job. He attended so many sick parades for which he swotted up symptoms at the local free library and once or twice fainted so realistically at work that the harassed and aged medical officer eventually capitulated and put him on light duties. He was given a job in the camp kitchen and every morning thereafter, lounging gracefully in the doorway of the kitchen hut, Ernie would make a point of watching as our sergeant marched us out to work on the railway.

The men I worked with were pacifists for different reasons. The majority of them were sincere and had registered from religious conviction of one kind or another. Some were shirkers who simply wanted to avoid war service, particularly duty overseas. Others had political views which made them regard the war as exploitation of the workers, or so they said. A very small number were pure cranks and their ingrown egos and passionate illogicalities made them hard to take. I remember one man, a member of a small religious sect, who was horror-stricken when he learned I was not only a Spiritualist but a medium, to boot. He refused to speak to me or to come within yards of me because he said I was 'of the Devil'. In our dormitory hut he would ostentatiously kneel beside his bunk and pray aloud to be delivered from 'the snares of Satan's servant' until the other men in the hut threw boots, brushes, anything they could lay their hands on, to make him shut up. After a few nights he disappeared from our hut altogether and peace reigned once more. Later we learned he had been sleeping in one of the outhouses until he had been discovered by a sergeant and reported to the Commanding Officer. When the C.O. questioned him about his curious behaviour the soldier said he would rather die than sleep in the same hut as 'a necromancer' and he got so excited about it that the C.O., a humane man, told him he would be moved to another dormitory. For a time we heard no more of our Brother until one day at pay parade he dramatically tore up the paper money and threw away the silver he had just been given as his pay, shouting that he would not take 'blood money'. This caused a sensation and one or two fingers got badly trampled in the scrum round his discarded silver. Soon afterwards the Brother was discharged from the army on psychiatric grounds and was seen no more. I was sorry for him, thinking he was sincere in his beliefs and the strain of army life had turned his brain, but Ernie was convinced the Brother had hit upon a brilliant way to 'work his ticket' and he was absolutely furious he had not thought of it first.

As a result of this episode I came in for a good deal of good-humoured kidding about Spiritualism and I was frequently challenged to 'produce a spirit now'. It was all meant as fun but it got to be repetitious and tiresome so one night after Lights Out in our dormitory hut when the 'chipping' started up again, I asked the men to relax and lie quietly in their bunks and perhaps someone might come to talk to them. After a few stifled giggles and embarrassed coughs, the men lay quietly and after a few minutes Mickey began to speak to them. He spoke to most of them individually giving them help and advice about various problems which I was unaware they had, and finally he introduced the sister of one of them who had passed on only a few weeks previously. The man and his dear sister were having a personal talk when one of the sergeants started to bang on the door of the hut and barged in to put one of the men on a charge for leaving some tools out in the rain, and our seance ended abruptly with the switching on of the overhead light. This caused the ectoplasm which the other side had taken from me to make the etheric larynx through which they speak to rush back into my body and I felt as though I had been kicked in the solar plexus. As I lay winded and retching, I remembered the warning Noah Zerdin had given me years before in the little café in Watford. For the first time in the practice of my mediumship I knew exactly what he meant. When I had recovered and the sergeant had taken himself off, the soldier who had been talking to his sister told the men in the hut he had not told a soul in the camp he had a sister, living or dead. There was no more kidding and I was often asked to give another seance in our hut but, fearing another kick in the midriff, I never did.

Long before we had finished our railway track, in the antic manner of the army a number of men including Ernie and me were transferred to a camp near Salisbury where the work consisted of making a new road near a big R.A.F. station.

Road-making is every bit as strenuous as laying a railway track but I preferred the new camp. I was often able to get home on week-end leave when I would give a group sitting on Saturday evening to people chosen by Edith as being in special need of my help. I was happy to carry on with my real work even if it was only in a small and restricted way.

For the first time since I had been in the army I met a fellow Spiritualist at the new camp. With several men I had been detailed to clear away broken road surface and we were working in the nerve-racking vicinity of a pneumatic drill when I became clairvoyantly aware of an elderly man standing close to one of the men working with me; the spirit man was as clear and life-like as the soldier whose attention he was trying to attract. In spite of the hideous distraction of the drill, I became aware the spirit wanted to tell the soldier he regretted his opposition to something. I felt diffident about passing on this message since for all I knew the soldier might share the point of view of the religious fanatic in the other camp. Then the drill ceased its exacerbating din for a few seconds and my rapport with the elderly spirit man grew until I knew beyond doubt he wanted to tell his son he was sorry he had been so antagonistic to his interest in Spiritualism but he knew better now. I had no reason to hesitate longer and as soon as the pneumatic drill paused again I told the soldier what I had seen and heard clairvoyantly. He introduced himself as Hubert Finnemore and said he recognised the description of his late father as an accurate one. He also confirmed that his father had been bitterly opposed to Spiritualism and there had been some ill-feeling between father and son on this account. Hubert was deeply touched that his father had made the effort to contact him through me in order to say he was sorry. We became friends and enjoyed many talks about our mutual interest in psychic matters. In fact Hubert and his wife are good friends of mine to this day.

The transfer from Shrewsbury suited me but it pleased my friend Ernie not at all. No longer was he able to watch the rest of us march out to the day's labour from the shelter of a cushy job. Ernie was now one of the marchers, and road-making appealed to him no more than laying sleepers. He began his sick parade routine and threw one or two impressive faints but the new Medical Officer was neither as aged nor as gullible as the old one, and he refused to certify Ernie as too fragile to work on the road in spite of all the symptoms Ernie produced for him.

After the failure of the sick parade ploy Ernie became very friendly with some members of an esoteric religious sect who used to meet in the evenings to read the Bible and sing hymns. Ernie attended these meetings and soon he was seldom to be seen without a Bible under his arm. One night over a cup of coffee in the NAAFI Ernie told me with great solemnity that he had been saved and, while he had no wish to hurt me, he knew now he could no longer be the friend of a man who had given his soul to the devil. This was familiar ground and I shook my head at him. 'It won't work, Ernie, not so soon after the last one, besides Sgt Grant was at Shrewsbury when it happened.' Ernie grinned disarmingly, 'I'd forgotten about Grant,' he said. 'Oh, well! I'll have to think of something else.' I suggested he might try resigning himself to the inevitable and he gave me a scathing look. 'I'm getting out of this shower if it's the last thing I do,' he said, 'in me prime of life an' I'm sweatin' for two bob a day. Ludicrous, that's wot it is! Up the Smoke if you knock off a few cases o' gin or somefink they queue up for it. At a fiver a bottle I'm tellin' you!' Ernie thumbed briskly through an invisible wad of fivers and kissed his fingers rapturously. He was a scoundrel; he was also kind, generous and lovable and I valued his friendship, so I bought him a beer and wished him luck.

By now Owen was on active service with a bomber squadron and Edith's letters were full of fears for him. I thought she would not be able to bear it if anything happened to Owen. There were other children of her first marriage who had left home long ago to marry and lead their own lives and though the bond between them and Edith was strong, Owen was her youngest and her best loved child. One morning I got a telegram to say he was wounded and in hospital near Canterbury. I was given seventy-two hours leave to go and be with my wife.

We sat on a bench outside Owen's ward in the hospital and waited for a doctor to come. We knew only that his aircraft had been badly hit by flak over Germany and he had barely managed to limp home where he had crash landed. We had no idea how badly he was hurt or even if he would live or die. We waited for an hour, two hours, and still no doctor came. I knew the hell Edith must be going through and I got very angry about what to me seemed a refinement of torture by the uncaring hospital staff. I started up to go and demand some-one's attention for my wife but Edith pulled me back with her gentle touch. 'There are so many anxious people, some of us must wait,' she said. I had under-estimated my wife, she was gold all through.

At last the doctor came and he was young and harassed and very weary. Owen had got off lightly though his sergeant had been killed. There were no broken bones, many superficial

cuts and bruises and a bad concussion. 'We'll have him back
with his squadron in less than a month,' said the young doctor
cheerfully. I saw the quiver of Edith's lip but she managed a
smile and said, 'That will please him, I know.'

When I got back to camp Ernie was nowhere to be seen. I
asked everyone I saw what had become of him and finally I
was told he had been sent to a psychiatric unit. It appeared
Ernie had bleached his hair one night while the rest of the
men in his hut were sleeping and had burst upon their astonished gaze the next morning as a radiant blond. He had then
rushed all round the camp screeching in a high falsetto that
he could not sleep another night in a hut with all those lovely
men or he would go crazy. Efforts to calm him down had been
met with hysterical laughter or floods of tears and finally two
medical orderlies had taken him off in a jeep to a destination
loosely described as 'the bin'. Since I knew Ernie's love life
was normal, and pretty busy at that, it was obvious this was a
new and somewhat desperate attempt to 'work his ticket'. I
have no idea whether his ploy succeeded but none of us saw
Ernie again.

When the new road was almost finished a notice went up on
the camp bulletin board asking for volunteers for bomb disposal duties. It was one of the elementary precepts of army
life never to volunteer for anything whatsoever and this invitation to play about with live bombs was regarded as a joke
in extremely poor taste. I am bound to say that for a long time
I passed the bulletin board daily without experiencing even
the smallest urge to inscribe my name in the space thoughtfully provided for the signatures of volunteers. This space
remained totally blank for many weeks. A day came when I
realised with a shock of annoyance that I was beginning to
feel a sense of personal guilt about this unanswered appeal. I
tried to argue myself out of this and my logic was impeccable,
but the feeling persisted and began seriously to disturb me. I
took to averting my eyes when I had to pass the bulletin
board, then I started to make detours so as to avoid it alto-

gether, but I could not rid myself of the nagging sense of guilt. I was led to question whether my contribution to the war effort was enough. Other men in their thousands were risking life and limb daily while *I* was making a road. Granted, the road was required for military purposes but I lived and worked in conditions considerably less dangerous than those of civilians in any of the big towns or cities; air-raids were few and far between in the Wiltshire wilds where our camp was located. One morning when I was making my usual detour to avoid the notice board I stopped in my tracks and without making any conscious decision to do so wheeled about and walked firmly to the bulletin board where I wrote my name in the space which had reproached me for so long and the moment it was done I was at peace with myself again.

In due course I was posted to a unit stationed in a large house in a residential part of Cardiff where I learned how to defuse unexploded bombs to render them harmless. Every man in this unit had volunteered to do this dangerous job and whether it was because we all faced the same dangers or because of a fortuitous blending of personalities there was great comradeship between us. In my bomb disposal days I encountered none of the bigotry which had condemned me out of hand because I was a Spiritualist medium. I was accepted as the person I was and for my part in the work of the unit. When first I arrived I had been appalled to find the major who was our Commanding Officer was dead keen on drill and parades and military discipline. It did not take me long to realise that discipline and trained co-ordination were the very factors on which our lives would depend when we became an operational unit. I tried very hard to overcome my parade ground apathy and eventually I was a passable soldier.

I made a number of friends in Cardiff who were kind enough to invite me to their homes in my free time and it was bliss to be in the atmosphere of a home again even though it was not my own. When the local Spiritualist church discovered who I was I was inundated with requests for sittings. I did what I could in my free time and it was a joy to experience again the satisfaction of giving help and reassurance to those in need of it.

By the time we were operational defusing a bomb was a disciplined routine and it had become second nature to do the right thing in the right way. Certainly we never lost our healthy respect for the bombs we handled but the precision with which the squad worked together and our total confidence in each other minimised both risk and nervous strain.

After many months the number of bombs our unit was called on to handle dwindled to vanishing point and we became idle and rather bored, missing the periodic stimulus of danger. There were rumours we were about to be disbanded and in fact eventually we were invited to volunteer for other forms of service because our training had been overtaken by new types of bombs and as a disposal unit we were obsolete.

Soon I was on my way to London for a three-month course in typing, shorthand and office routine. As the train rushed through the countryside I indulged in a daydream. There was a general who was not unlike the victor of Alamein and he was studying a map. Sometimes he sat at an imposing desk, at other times he was roughing it in a caravan; but wherever he was he was surrounded by officers who wore red tabs on their uniforms. Impatiently he waved the officers away. Flint will take care of it, he said. This was my cue to enter the dream with my neat dispatch case. In a later version I acquired red tabs, too. This embellishment made me laugh until I almost choked and an elderly man sitting opposite asked if he should thump me on the back. For the rest of the journey I contented myself with dwelling pleasurably on the thought that while I was on my course in Holborn I was to be allowed to live at home.

For years I had been a two-finger hunt and peck typist and I was quite proud of my speed. On the first day of the course I was chagrined to learn I had been doing it all wrong and thenceforth I must use all my fingers and be a touch typist.

They gave me a diagram of the typewriter keyboard to prop up in front of me and dutifully I started to learn these new ways. Filing too had a lot more in it than I had ever suspected. It was by no means the simple matter of putting papers in a box in alphabetical order which I had hitherto supposed it was. There were drawers, sliding panels, tags of different colours, cards, folders, indexes and the filing of one simple letter was a nightmare operation in which, it seemed to me, the simple letter was lost for ever. As for shorthand, I found the hieroglyphs baffling enough without the complications of heavy and light strokes, dots and dashes and all the rest. If it had not been for the happiness of living at home and the fact that I had my evenings and week-ends to myself I think I would have given up in despair of ever making head or tail of it all, but I soldiered on with the threat of the end of course examination hanging over my head like Thingummy's sword.

Our home circle had resumed its regular sittings now that I was at home and one evening a woman's voice spoke in an agitated way, asking to speak to her son. We asked her for her name and she said it was Clara Novello Davies. One of the sitters remarked that she must be Ivor Novello's mother. The woman in spirit said she *was* Ivor Novello's mother and she was extremely anxious to speak to him. We explained to this spirit we did not know her son but if there was some message she wanted to convey to him we would make every effort to see he got it. The spirit thanked us for our offer but said she wanted to speak to her son personally because what she wanted to say was too private for any ears but his own. Naturally we wondered why Ivor Novello's mother sounded so distressed, but after she had gone we thought no more about it. Some weeks later an actor friend of mine asked me to give a seance at his flat because he was anxious to help one of his friends who had become interested in Spiritualism. I agreed to give the seance and when I arrived at his flat on the evening we had arranged I was introduced to his friend who turned out to be the enchanting Beatrice Lillie. Almost as soon as the lights were turned out Miss Lillie's son David who had been lost on active service with the navy spoke to her and they had a happy reunion. When David had gone I was surprised to hear the voice of Clara Novello Davies addressing Bea Lillie. She asked Miss Lillie to contact Ivor and arrange for him to sit with me so that she could talk to him about something very urgent. Miss Lillie asked Novello's mother to say something which she could repeat to Ivor so that he would know it was really his mother who was speaking. The spirit said that Ivor had that moment entered his flat from Oxford where he had been to visit a former teacher of his. As soon as the lights were turned on Bea Lillie telephoned Ivor Novello and told him all that had occurred at the sitting. She found that what his mother had said about his having just returned from visiting a teacher in Oxford was true and Novello showed a great deal of interest. It was arranged there and then on the telephone that I should give him a sitting in his flat one night after his show *The Dancing Years*.

On the night I was to give Ivor Novello his sitting I met my actor friend at the Ivy restaurant where he had invited me to dine. We were to meet Ivor after his show and go with him to his flat. While we were having dinner Ivor phoned through to the Ivy and cancelled the arrangement. Both my friend and I were disappointed and also somewhat annoyed at being put off at such short notice without a very convincing excuse. My friend thought Ivor had probably had cold feet at the thought of speaking to spirits in his own flat and probably imagined it would be haunted thereafter. We got over our mild 'peeve' and enjoyed an excellent wartime dinner. Some weeks afterwards we read in the papers that Ivor was to be prosecuted for an offence in connection with petrol rationing. Evidently he had been driving down to his country home at week-ends using petrol which some girl fan had wangled for him without realising he was committing what at that period of the war was a criminal offence. Then it became clear to me why Clara Novello Davies had made such efforts to contact her son, obviously she wanted to warn him against accepting this illicit petrol. If Ivor had not cancelled his sitting with me at the last moment as he did it is possible he might have avoided the shame and misery he suffered when later he served a month in gaol.

I met Ivor Novello some years after these events and he sat with me many times. Often his mother would come to speak to him. Ivor told me that once during his prison sentence he was sitting in his cell one evening feeling low and depressed and wondering if he could endure his sentence without a mental breakdown when his mother appeared to him. He said she looked as real and living as in life and the look of love and encouragement on her face gave him the strength to carry on and saved his reason.

I was in the theatre on the night when Ivor gave his first performance of *The Dancing Years* after he came out of prison and it was a night to remember; the whole house rose to him and the applause went on and on until it seemed the audience would never let him go. It was a wonderful night, a great theatrical occasion, and it gave Ivor the assurance he needed that the past was behind him and he was still loved.

Beatrice Lillie sat with me a number of times after her first sitting and once Rudolph Valentino came to speak to her. He mentioned their meeting in Hollywood and Miss Lillie asked him if he could remember the circumstances of it. Valentino said it was at a beach party at the home of Constance Talmadge and he spoke of a photograph which was taken on this occasion in which Bea Lillie appeared and Valentino was sitting on a fence with his arm round Pola Negri. After this sitting Miss Lillie told me the beach party was the only time she had met Rudolph Valentino and the photograph he had described was at that moment in a trunk in her apartment in New York.

The sword of Damocles inevitably descended and I sat the end of course examination designed to weed out those without aptitude for office duties. I never had got the hang of their filing system or mastered the hieroglyphs of shorthand and I still used my two-finger hunt and peck method on the typewriter in preference to the ten-finger exercise. Needless to say I was weeded out and the unlikely picture of the *éminence grise* behind the general's desk vanished for ever.

While I was still licking my wounds I was told men were urgently needed in the mines to ensure the nation's coal supply and too few volunteers were coming forward in response to appeals. Rashly I responded to these unsubtle hints and in no time at all I was sitting in a train on my way to Wolverhampton to train as a miner. For some reason which doubtless I was told at the time it was not possible to remain in the army if you were a miner so before entraining for Wolverhampton I had become a civilian again.

What I failed to take into account when I let myself be talked into ensuring the nation's coal supply was the fact that during the relatively short periods I had been enclosed in my cabinet during the public demonstrations of my mediumship invariably I had suffered from claustrophobia to a greater or lesser degree depending on the size of the cabinet and how airless it was. The symptoms were unpleasant but not so severe as seriously to disconcert me and I had been able to put up with them for the duration of the seances. Foolishly I did not consider the possibility that working in the bowels of the earth for hours at a stretch would be likely to induce these symptoms but a thousand times worse.

During the training period I tried hard to control the feelings of being trapped and stifled and the unreasoning terrors which assailed me every time I descended to the coal face, but as the weeks dragged on it became more and more obvious I could never be a miner and every hour underground was an unspeakable torture. When I could stand it no longer I was returned with thanks to the army and posted forthwith to a big camp not far from Liverpool docks. Our work consisted of loading heavy crates of supplies for the forces overseas on to lorries which took them to the docks for shipment abroad. Though the work was hard and exhausting and the camp seemed to be some kind of special target for night raids and daytime flying bombs it was positive bliss after the horror of working in the mine. I remained there contentedly enough until V-E Day.

Ten

IN January 1946 a few days after my thirty-fifth birthday I swapped my army uniform for the civilian outfit thoughtfully provided by a paternal government and walked out of the demobilisation centre with a railway ticket for home and freedom in my pocket.

As I opened the front door of No. 31 with my key Edith was coming out of the kitchen with a freshly made pot of tea in her hands. She was so excited to see me she dumped the teapot on the polished top of the hall table and rushed into my arms. For years the mark made by the scalding teapot remained to remind us of that reunion and neither of us could ever bear to have the stain removed. Later that same day Owen now a flight-lieutenant wearing the ribbon of the D.F.C. on his tunic turned up unexpectedly on leave and the family was complete. In our house happiness was always shared with friends and we telephoned to invite several to celebrate with us. I went to the local wine store to see what I could buy for their entertainment, not expecting much, for supplies of wine and spirits had started to dry up early in the war and by this time were in very short supply indeed. The keeper of the store was a man who had occasionally attended my group seances. Before I could even ask for the bottle of wine I wanted to buy he produced with a flourish a magnum of champagne. He told me it was the last of his stock and he had kept it for the day I came home for good, nor would he allow me to pay for it.

Late that night when the toasts had been drunk and our friends had gone, under the overhead light I saw the new lines which the war had etched on Edith's face. Years of uncertainty, constant anxiety about Owen, and sleepless nights while bombs dropped all round the house had taken their toll. She looked old and tired, but to me she had never seemed as beautiful.

I allowed myself a few days to get acclimatised to civilian life, then the doors of the Temple of Light were opened again and I resumed the work I was born to do.

At one group seance where Air Chief Marshal Lord Dowding, a convinced Spiritualist, was an honoured guest, my Cockney guide, Mickey, introduced a young airman in these words: 'There's a chap here from the Air Force who wants to get in touch with his parents. He's so excited I don't know if he will manage to speak but I'll try to help him.' Shortly we heard the voice of the airman asking us to contact his father and mother. He had been to see them often, he said, but they could not see him. He told us he was killed when his plane crashed over Norway when he was twenty years old and he was his parents' only son. 'Please tell Mother I'm all right now,' he urged, 'she is so unhappy it is making her ill.'

No one in the group could identify this communicator so Mr Walter J. West, our Vice-President at the Temple of Light, asked for the boy's full name and address and promised to get in touch with the parents if it were possible to do so. 'Thank you so much,' replied the dead boy, 'I had three Christian names, Peter William Handford and my surname was Kite.' He then gave an address in Grange Park, north London, where he said his parents were still living. But that was not all, Peter Kite next spoke to a man in the group saying, 'I know you, you are Mr Turner, you took out my tooth.' None of the other sitters knew Mr Turner was a dentist nor did they know his name. Mr Turner said he remembered Peter Kite coming to him for treatment some years before but he did not know he had been killed nor even that he had joined the R.A.F.

After the seance Mr West went to Grange Park and found the house where Peter Kite had said his parents lived. The dead boy's mother, Mrs May Kite, answered the door to Mr West's ring and when she heard what he had to tell her she readily accepted an invitation to attend a special group seance at the Temple of Light with Peter's father.

Because we felt Lord Dowding's presence at the first seance had helped Flight Lieutenant Peter Kite to manifest we invited him to be a member of the special group at which the boy's parents would be guests and he readily agreed to sit with us.

Almost as soon as the light was turned off Mickey came to tell us Conan Doyle wanted to say a few words to Mr and Mrs Kite before their son came to speak to them. Doyle, who in his lifetime finally became convinced of Spiritualism after years of sitting with mediums, then spoke very sympathetically to the parents who had no knowledge of psychic matters. He explained to them how after Peter's plane crashed he had found himself alive in a new more subtle body which resembled in every respect his physical body which he could see lying motionless in the wreckage of his aircraft. At first, Doyle told the couple, their son had been bewildered because although he could see the body which he recognised as himself he felt so gloriously alive and well he simply did not realise he was dead. When two peasants came to investigate the wrecked plane Peter was puzzled when they seemed neither to see nor hear him, but soon some friends of his whom he knew to be dead came to explain his new condition of life to him and to take him to his new plane of being.

As soon as Conan Doyle had finished speaking Peter Kite excitedly greeted his father and mother. 'I've got the dog, Mother,' he said laughingly, 'it's an Alsatian.' This was a reference to a joke he had played on his mother only a few days before his death. Peter had been fond of dogs and he had telephoned his mother to say he was sending home an Alsatian he had acquired. Mrs Kite was not a dog lover and the thought of a huge Alsatian tearing round her house had appalled her. After teasing her for a while Peter had relented and reminded her it was 1 April.

'I saw you putting my photograph in your bag with the ones from Norway before you left home,' went on the spirit voice. Mrs Kite told us she had changed her handbag before leaving for the seance and had transferred its contents including her son's photograph and some which had recently been sent to her of his grave in Norway.

'You are keeping the garden in good trim,' said Peter. 'I like the part you have made into a garden of memories. Do you know the birds nesting in the cherry tree can see me even if you cannot?' The parents told us that six years before when Peter was killed they had apportioned a patch of garden as a memorial to him and in it they had planted a cherry tree in which birds were building nests at that time. 'I often go to my room and you haven't changed a single thing in it.' Peter continued. 'My model plane is still there and all my books and that wallpaper I didn't like!' It was true that the parents had kept their son's room exactly as it had been on the day he was killed and he had never cared for the wallpaper in it. 'I'm glad my car is still going but it's a bit small for you, Dad, isn't it?' Mr Kite agreed Peter's sports car fitted him a little too snugly; he was a large and somewhat overweight man. 'I'm saying all these silly little things so you will know it's really me speaking and that I do come to see you, above all I want you and Mother to know I am alive, more alive now than I ever was.'

For close on forty minutes the voice of Peter Kite went on piling evidential detail on detail, details trivial in themselves but in the aggregate giving his parents incontrovertible proof of his identity and his continued existence.

When the seance was over both parents declared their son's survival of death had been conclusively proved to them. 'I

143

never thought very much about this kind of thing before,' said Mr Kite, 'but now I am completely convinced.' Mrs Kite added, 'I have found more comfort in this seance than I have got from any other source since my son was killed and I have lost a great deal of the bitterness I felt.'

During one of my leaves from the army I had given a sitting to Mrs Marie Barrat, a Belgian lady living in Golders Green, whose son George had been killed on active service early in the war. George had manifested at her sitting and had given such undeniable proof of his survival that her grief had been assuaged and life had become worth living again. Mrs Barrat was wealthy and she had a generous heart. As a sort of 'thank-you' combined with a memorial to her son, she decided to give other mothers who had lost sons the opportunity to receive the comfort she had been given. As soon as I returned home after my army service Mrs Barrat booked a regular seance with me and to it she would bring mothers from all over the country, their expenses being paid from a fund she established for the purpose.

Before each of her seances Mrs Barrat would tell her mothers that she had told the medium nothing whatsoever about any of them, not even their names, so that any evidence obtained might be the more valuable. Many touching reunions took place at these sittings and mothers went away comforted.

Once one of Mrs Barrat's mothers did not turn up at the time the seance was due to begin and after waiting for a few minutes we decided we must sit without her. When the seance had been in progress for a while a young man's voice was heard asking for his mother. Mrs Barrat asked him who he was and when he had given her his name she realised he must be the son of the missing mother. Mrs Barrat explained to the dead boy that his mother had not come and the seance was being held without her. 'Mother's train was late,' said the voice, 'but she is here now. She is sitting on a chair on the landing outside this room. Please let me talk to her.' Regretfully Mrs Barrat told the boy she could not open the door of the seance room to admit his mother in case the light from outside harmed the medium. 'I must try to speak to her somehow,' said the young man, 'she grieves for me so incessantly it makes me very unhappy and I can't settle down in my new life here.' Then a wonderful thing happened. As a rule the voices of the discarnate speak from a point above my head slightly to one side of me within what Mickey has referred to as my 'auric emanation', but as this spirit spoke his voice moved right away from me across the room to the door where he called loudly for his mother. From outside the door the mother answered him and the dead boy and the living mother talked together through the door until the woman was convinced he was really her own son alive and loving as he was in life.

At another group it was a daughter who returned to comfort her mother. A Mrs Maxon who lived in Oxford telephoned one afternoon, on impulse as she told me, and since there happened to be a vacant place in one of the groups she was given the seat. Her daughter manifested and spoke of her career as a dancing teacher in a clear girlish voice with a tinge of north-country accent. The girl reminded her mother of the last ballet they had seen together at Covent Garden, *Les Sylphides*, and told her that since her passing she had met Anna Pavlova for whom she had always had the greatest respect and admiration as being the head of her own profession. The daughter also spoke of a time when she had played truant from school years before and waited three hours in the snow for a seat in the gallery to see Pavlova dance at a matinée. Mickey was puzzled about a dress he said the girl was wearing. First he said it was a wedding dress, then he thought it might be a confirmation dress, but when he described some red flowers on the skirt Mrs Maxon at once recognised it as the long ballet dress worn for *Les Sylphides* and she told us that she had herself sewn the red flowers on to the skirt some time before her daughter's last illness. 'I have been given absolute proof of the survival of my daughter,' wrote Mrs Maxon in a letter to *Psychic News* after this seance, 'I was a perfect stranger at the seance. I booked my seat by telephone from Oxford and I was alone.'

Most of those who communicate from the other side at my seances speak of how happy they are in their new condition of life, but I remember one entity who startled one of my groups by being very peevish and disgruntled. He told us he was an American G.I. who had been killed in a London 'blitz' and when a lady member of the group said she was surprised to hear him talk in that way he replied, 'Well, it wasn't any fun to come all the way over to London just to die in a raid!'

The direct voice seance normally has two restrictions imposed on it. One is that it must be held in absolute darkness. The other, that only a limited number of sitters may be present. Both before the war and during the war when I was on leave Noah Zerdin and his circle had been experimenting with a specially constructed cabinet in which I sat during seances in an effort to lift both these restrictions. Eventually these experiments were so successful that it was decided to celebrate the fifteenth anniversary of the founding of The Link Association with a huge public seance in the Kingsway Hall at which the Hall would be fully lit and the audience would number more than a thousand people.

On the big night Air Chief Marshal Lord Dowding introduced me to the audience and asked them to accept his personal assurance that no fraud would take place. The cabinet, about seven feet high and four feet square, was placed in the centre of the platform where it could be seen by everyone in the audience. Those at the extreme ends of the gallery could probably see all round it. The four sides of the cabinet were covered in with tarpaulin to ensure no light could enter and I sat inside on an ordinary chair. In front of the cabinet at a distance of eighteen to twenty inches stood a microphone and the members of the Zerdin circle sat round it in the form of an ellipse with the cabinet as focal point. In these conditions, under the full glare of the hall's lighting the huge audience was given a demonstration of the independent direct voice comparable to those experienced as a rule only by small groups sitting in privacy.

Mickey's clear Cockney voice was the first to be heard that evening and since it seems to be part of his function to put people at their ease before a seance he raised a laugh by saying perkily, 'Proper crowd 'ere tonight, ain't there? I expect a lot of 'em don't know much about this kind of thing but I'll do my best for 'em!' and from then on he did indeed.

The first visitor from the other side gave his name as Roy Marchant and was acknowledged by his parents in the audience. 'Hello, Mother! Hello, Dad,' said Roy excitedly. 'I want you to know I am not dead, I'm marvellously alive and I send all my love to you and to baby.' His parents replied affectionately. Then Roy thanked his mother for a children's party she had given for his child. 'Don't think of me as being a long way off,' he went on. 'I'm not. I am often with you, I was with you in Switzerland! There isn't any real separation.'

The next communicator gave her name as Gladys Richmond and spoke to a man in the front of the audience pleading to be forgiven for some misunderstanding between them when she was on earth. 'I'm sorry about everything,' she said, 'it was an accident – you do believe that, don't you?' The man assured her he both believed and understood. 'I'm so happy you understand,' said Gladys, 'and that you realise I love you and one day we will be together again. You often read that last letter I wrote to you before I went to Scotland, I can see you reading it.'

'I feel like an interloper, but I hope you won't mind,' came the voice of a woman. 'I am Stella Patrick Campbell and I want to introduce Leslie Howard to you.' There was a rustle of expectancy throughout the auditorium. Leslie Howard, the famous actor, had been killed three years before when his unarmed plane was shot down by a German fighter and his death had been widely mourned.

A cultured masculine voice was heard. 'God bless you! I

am happy to be able to come and speak to you in this way. Many of you do not perhaps understand fully that there is no death. Those of us over here who come in this way, come to guide and help you, to try to uplift you. Spirit guidance does not cease, that which happened two thousand years ago has happened through the centuries and it is still happening today. I went to meetings like this when I was on earth and I found great comfort and interest. I was not, perhaps, a Spiritualist but certainly I believed in man's survival of death.' Speaking on a more personal note the voice of Howard went on: 'I would like to speak to Phyllis James, my former secretary.' Miss James answered him and he asked her to send his love to 'Ruth' and to tell his family of his appearance that night. 'Death has not robbed me of any of my faculties,' he concluded, 'God bless each one of you here tonight.'

One of the most touching contacts of the evening began very quietly with Mickey saying: 'I want to speak to the lady all in grey at the back because her boy's here. He was in the navy. His name is Jim.' A woman at the very back of the gallery called: 'Is it for me?' The moment her voice was heard, suddenly and loudly came the pathetic cry: 'Mum! Mum! I'm so glad you've come!' 'Darling, darling!' was all the mother could reply. 'I'm not dead you know,' Jim assured her anxiously, 'I'm all right!' In trying to bring conviction Jim's anxiety increased. 'I wasn't drowned. 'I'm ALIVE!' The shouted word rang through the hall, fraught with the pain of not knowing whether the comfort he sought to bring would be fully understood. Mickey intervened at this point to provide the anticlimax which restored a smile to every face. 'Jim's a darned sight more alive than you are, lady, I'll tell you!'

When the seance was nearly over a woman's voice was heard speaking in the cultured and precise diction so familiar to my own home circle, the voice of Ellen Terry. 'Ladies and Gentlemen,' she said, 'I was asked to come and speak here tonight for a few moments though I know too well many have

148

more proficiency than I. For all of you who have faith in the spirit and the surety of knowledge that life continues after death there is no reason why you should not develop the great gifts of the spirit in your own homes. Sometimes you may get despondent and depressed and feel you are not making sufficient progress; we help you from our side all we can though we cannot say how long individual development will take. With some it takes years, with others it comes very quickly if they persevere; but have faith, sit in sincerity of spirit and use your gifts to serve mankind. The aftermath of war has left the world in chaos, more than ever will you be needed to transmit the help that can come from our side of life. Man's ignorance and selfishness has brought great suffering to mankind, and people say, "Why does God allow these things?" but God gave you free will. Search to find a link with those in spirit and remember the promise of Jesus when you sit, "Lo, I am with you always." Go forward in strength and know that you, too, will be serving. Be His servants, His children, and it will bring to you the peace which is everlasting.'

With these words the first big public demonstration of the independent direct voice held in full light came to an end; it had been successful beyond all our hopes and it was only the first of many more I was to give not only in London but in the largest halls all over the country, and I felt more than ever assured that my life was to be devoted to comforting those who mourn and giving certainty to those seeking to know what lies beyond the illusion we call death.

After that evening letters poured into the Temple of Light by the sackful. So many people wanted to sit with me privately or to join group seances, so many societies all over England wanted me to demonstrate my mediumship, that it became abundantly clear I would have to restrict severely the amount of work I did or I would risk a nervous breakdown and possibly as a consequence lose my precious gift altogether. To this end the Temple of Light was reorganised and all matters of finance and administration were taken out of my hands by the Committee so that I would be free from worry and anxiety and my work could be arranged in such a way that my mediumship would be used to help as many people as possible without overtaxing my strength or my nervous system. The Rev. Arthur Sharp resigned his living at St Stephen's, Hampstead, to become our president and the Rev. Charles Drayton Thomas joined the committee. It was a wonderful band which gathered round me at that time full of enthusiasm.

At another demonstration in full light, this time at the La Scala Theatre, London, a voice purporting to be that of John Wesley delivered a wonderful oration in which he told the audience of the spirit world's plan to bring light to our darkened world and to spread the truth of life after death. As I sat in my stuffy cabinet on the stage and listened to him I marvelled at his eloquence and mastery of language so far beyond the limits of my own education.

When Wesley's voice faded and after various entities had spoken to friends in the audience the voice of a young girl was heard excited and apparently overcome with emotion. Her words halting but clear, she said it was her first attempt to communicate.

'What is your name?' asked Drayton Thomas who was sitting on the stage with Lord Dowding and my home circle. 'My name is Doreen,' the girl answered. 'Can you tell us your other name?' was the next question. As though the girl found it too difficult to speak Mickey answered for her that her surname was Marshall. There was a buzz of excitement from the audience as they speculated whether Doreen Marshall could be one of the victims of the perverted killer Neville Heath who had been hanged for the murder of another unfortunate girl not long before.

'Did anyone here know Doreen Marshall?' Drayton Thomas asked the audience. A man somewhere near the front answered that he lived opposite her home. Then the girl tried to speak again. 'I am all right now,' she said, then speaking to the man who had claimed to be a neighbour, 'I used to pat your dog.' By that time the girl's emotion was too overwhelming and the link was broken. As I listened to the audience still buzzing with excited comment I could not help feeling sad that the efforts of this poor murdered girl to communicate had apparently had an effect so much greater than the whole of the fine oration spoken by the voice claiming to be John Wesley.

When Owen was demobbed he went back to his old job at Elstree Studios, but as the weeks passed both Edith and I noticed with concern he was not the happy-go-lucky young man he was before the war. He was restless and unsettled and he had taken to spending his evenings shut away in his room instead of going out with his friends to enjoy himself as he used to do. I supposed this uncharacteristic behaviour was the result of years of strain as a bomber pilot and made allowances for the unaccountable mood swings and the flashes of irritability which were so unlike his old self. Remembering the concussion after his crash landing we would ask anxiously if he suffered from headaches or blurred vision or symptoms of vertigo. The object of our solicitude would answer with exasperated sighs or a resigned casting up of the eyes to heaven. Edith began to talk rather glibly about neuroses and the splitting of personalities under stress and I discovered she was taking textbooks on psychology out of the local free library and was hiding them behind cushions on the sitting-room chairs when Owen or I were about.

The answer to Owen's malaise turned out to be simpler than any which had occurred to his mother. During a period of flight training in California he had fallen in love with an American girl. They had corresponded throughout the war and as soon as he was back in civilian life Owen had written to her proposing marriage. Since he had been completely honest about his financial prospects which were less than dazzling and his girl was the daughter of wealthy parents Owen waited for her answer on tenterhooks, alternating between euphoric hope and the blackest despair. As soon as she cabled to say she was taking the first available boat to England to marry him Owen was himself again.

Owen and Jane were married by Father Sharp in his former church of St Stephen's, Hampstead. Jane was a beautiful bride and Owen a very proud bridegroom. What remained of Owen's squadron formed a guard of honour and since the bride's parents were unable to travel to England for the ceremony I stood *in loco parentis* and gave Jane away. It was a happy wedding even if the bridegroom's mother shed a few tears as the couple left for their honeymoon on the coast.

Later they settled in a small flat in Maida Vale and in due course a daughter was born who gave Edith and the young parents great joy.

When the blow fell it was sudden. We had been out to dinner with friends and it had been a happy evening. On the way home in the tube Edith remarked she felt rather strange and when I looked at her under the train lights her face was grey. I wanted to telephone for the doctor as soon as we got home but Edith would have none of him so I gave her some brandy which put the colour back into her face and reassured me.

It was dawn when I awoke with a start, feeling uneasy. I looked at Edith and she seemed to be peacefully sleeping. The feeling of unease persisted, and I looked more closely at her. One corner of her mouth was drooping. I sprang out of bed and ran to the telephone. When the doctor came he told me Edith had suffered a stroke. From the gay bright personality she had been, my wife was suddenly helpless and her long illness of five years' duration had begun.

A married daughter of Edith's helped me over the first most difficult period by nursing her mother devotedly, but the time soon came when she and her husband and family had to move to another district and I had to manage as best I could on my own.

Although I am able to talk to those who guide and help me

152

from the other side as easily as my sitters do, I do not usually ask for help with material problems because they have always made it very clear I must not expect my life to be easy nor must I imagine I am entitled to special privileges because I am their medium. But when the shopping, the cooking, the care of my wife and trying to do my spiritual work at the same time became a burden of almost nightmare proportions I decided to ask them for help. At the next sitting of my home circle I asked for someone to be sent to my assistance.

'Someone has already been sent,' said Mickey, 'he is working in this house and he was at your last big meeting at the Kingsway Hall.' I could not imagine what Mickey meant. The only person working in the house was a young fellow who was redecorating one of the bedrooms.

'You can't mean the painter?' I said to Mickey. 'Yes I do,' he answered perkily. 'His name is Bill Willis and he is wondering what on earth to do when he finishes the job here because the partner he had has walked out on him. Ask him and he will take over your worries and become interested in your work.' It was true there had originally been two painters when the job was started and for the past few days one of them had been missing but even so Mickey's solution to my problems seemed highly unlikely. 'Ask him! I'm telling you, he'll do it,' said Mickey with a trace of impatience at my obvious incredulity. 'Very well,' I said. 'If you say so, Mickey.'

The next morning very diffidently I took a cup of tea into the room where the painter was working alone. To check on Mickey's statement, I was about to ask him if he had been at my Kingsway Hall meeting when he told me how interesting he had found it. He told me he had sat next to a woman whose son, killed in the war, had spoken to her in a voice the woman had told Bill was exactly his voice when he was on earth. 'Is it really true?' said Bill, 'It's almost too wonderful to be really so.' I assured him it was true, then, testing Mickey further, I asked if his partner had left him in the lurch. 'Yes,' said Bill.

'He has left me in a right old mess. I can't carry on this business without another fellow and he's walked out for good. I don't know what I'll do when I finish this job. Get a job in a factory, most likely.'

'Would you like to come and work here?' I asked. 'I need someone to run the house and help me to care for my wife.'

Bill hesitated, then asked if a room went with the job. When I said it did, he offered to try it out if I did not mind being experimented upon while he learned to cook. He also said he would like to know more about 'this spirit business'.

Soon it was obvious Bill was a treasure. Quickly he mastered such routine as we had in our house and began to study cookery books and then to serve up delicious and imaginative meals. He became devoted to Edith and fussed over her like a hen with one chick. He also did all he could to make life easier for me and soon he was a regular sitter in my home circle and in due time someone he had known and loved on the other side came to speak to him and gave him his personal conviction of survival. Many of my friends and sitters will remember Bill with affection before his sadly premature death from an inoperable cancer.

The Committee of the Temple of Light organised another huge demonstration in the Kingsway Hall. As on the former occasion I was to sit in my stuffy cabinet on the stage while the hall would be fully lighted. Weeks before the advertised date all available seats were booked and on the night itself hundreds had to be turned away at the doors and all standing room was taken.

As usual Mickey spoke first, but this time, unusually, he told the huge audience that Mickey was only the name by which he was known in the world of spirit and to his medium. He said that in his life on earth he was called John Whitehead and he had sold newspapers outside Camden Town underground station until he was run over and killed by a lorry when he was ten years old. 'I'm a lot happier over here than I ever was on your side,' he assured the crowded hall, 'you could say kicking the bucket was the best thing I ever did!' This caused a general laugh and tension throughout the hall relaxed noticeably.

The next spirit voice claimed to be 'Jack Hickinbottom, who used to live at 76 Albert Street, Tipton, Staffordshire'. From the gallery a woman's voice answered, 'Yes, son, I am here!' Mother and son then talked together over the illusory gulf of death about such trivialities as the colour of a mackintosh, the name of a neighbour's dog and the nature of the son's last illness, all of which in themselves of no importance whatsoever, but to the mother who had travelled from her home in the Midlands only that morning and knew no one in London they provided convincing evidence that it was actually to her son, dead for eight years, she was speaking.

At the end of the meeting the Rev. Drayton Thomas gave a short address in which he tried to impress on the audience that there was more in these demonstrations of ours than the fact of communication between this world and the next; scientific, domestic and emotional proof were all very well, he said, but if that were all that was taken away from the meeting then the orange had been peeled and the fruit thrown away. 'The real meaning of it all,' he went on, 'is life moving onwards from level to level and ever reaching up to God.'

A few days later the following letter appeared in *Psychic News*:

A number of the audience at Kingsway Hall attending the Temple of Light direct-voice demonstrations appear to wonder if the public address equipment is quite genuine. Being the engineer responsible for the equipment, I can assure these people that the apparatus is installed on the Saturday morning, several hours before any official of the organisation arrives. It is tested by myself, and during the whole of the meeting the microphones are under my sole control.

Five standard velocity type microphones are used, the

two in front of the cabinet being wired back to the amplifier separately. The one used by the chairman and the one at the side of the table are uni-directional, i.e. will only pick up a signal from the front and are wired in parallel. A ribbon desk type microphone with a switch is put at the other end of the table and is only 'alive' when the switch is depressed. This is used for asking people in the hall to speak up or to give an explanation during the demonstration. It should be noted that if the switch is used, an immediate automatic indication is given to me. It is quite impossible to use this microphone secretly.

The microphones in front of the cabinet are switched on a few minutes after the medium has entered and at the same time the table mikes are switched off and are not put on again until the control indicates he has finished. This leaves only the two cabinet mikes which can possibly pick up any signal.

Frankly, when I first installed this equipment some time ago I did not expect these microphones to pick up very much, if anything at all, because in between them and the medium is a curtain of fairly thick material and if the reader would like to try a simple experiment, let him hang a towel over a radio set when someone is talking. Of course it goes muffled and similarly the voice of Mickey should be the same but as everyone who has heard it knows, it is not so.

Now! And this is important, I am not a Spiritualist or a personal friend of any of the officials nor do I know any of the staff of *Psychic News* but I should like two questions answered.

Is the voice inside or outside the cabinet? If inside, why so clear?

Why don't people in the immediate vicinity of the cabinet hear what is going into the mikes, because in order to get the result that is obtained it is necessary to speak about two feet away in a voice about twice as loud as normal conversational level? It makes you think.

The letter was signed by Mr George A. Muirhead of 99 Drewstead Road, London, S.W.16, at that time a sound engineer with the Tannoy Public Address Equipment Company.

Eleven

WHILE the Rev. Charles Drayton Thomas served on the committee of the Temple of Light and was a member of my own home circle, he wore quite a different hat as a member of the Council of the Society for Psychical Research. This Society was founded in 1882 by a group of scholars and scientists whose avowed purpose was 'to make a systematic investigation of certain phenomena which appear inexplicable on any generally recognised hypothesis', and as a body the S.P.R. is generally considered to be the most sceptical in the world. However, once Drayton Thomas had been convinced by various stringent tests of his own that the phenomena produced by my mediumship were not only genuine but of a high order he had the courage of his conviction and appeared on the platform at many of my demonstrations to testify publicly to the reality of the voices.

It came to Dray's ears that some of his colleagues in the S.P.R. who had attended one of my demonstrations were suggesting the voices were produced by my lips though they thought I might be obtaining the messages clairaudiently. Dray was determined to devise a test which if successful would dispose of this suggestion once and for all. Naturally I agreed to whatever test conditions he laid down as I have always agreed to co-operate when I felt a researcher was honest, sincere and open-minded. As to the outcome of Drayton Thomas' experimental test, I cannot do better than quote

158

from the account of it which was published under his By-line in the *Psychic News* of 14 February 1948.

On February 5, I placed over his tightly closed lips a strip of Elastoplast. It was $5\frac{1}{2}$ inches long and $2\frac{1}{2}$ inches wide and very strongly adhesive. This I pressed firmly over and into the crevices of the closed lips. A scarf was then tied tightly over this and the medium's hands tied firmly to the arms of his chair; another cord was so tied that he would be unable to bend down his head. Thus, supposing he endeavoured during trance to loosen the bandage, it would be quite impossible for him to reach it.

Anyone can discover by tightly closing the lips and trying to speak how muffled and unintelligible are the sounds then produced. My experiment was designed to show that under the above conditions clearly enunciated speech and plenty of it could be produced by the direct voice. The experiment was entirely successful. Voices were soon speaking with their usual clarity and Mickey emphasised his ability several times by shouting loudly. Some twelve persons were present and we all heard more than enough to convince the most obdurate sceptic that the sealing of Mr Flint's mouth in no way prevented unseen speakers from saying anything they wished. At the close of the sitting I examined the cords and the plaster, finding all intact and undisturbed. The plaster was so strongly adhering I had considerable difficulty in removing it without causing pain.

Not long after this account appeared in print I gave a demonstration in the Kingsway Hall and when my part of it was over Drayton Thomas described this test and its successful outcome to the two thousand people in the audience.

Dray was very anxious to repeat his test in the presence of the Research Officer of the S.P.R. at that time Dr D. J. West. I agreed to co-operate and so on 7 May 1948 Dray brought Dr

West and three other guests to my seance room at Sydney Grove.

After Dr West and Mr Denys Parsons, an S.P.R. colleague of his, had examined the cabinet to make certain no microphone or other apparatus was concealed in it, I took my place inside sitting on an ordinary upright chair. Dr West and Mr Parsons then strapped my extended arms to the side posts of my chair, then bound round each arm to the chair by winding a long thread of embroidery silk round and round. They then put adhesive plaster across my lips, two strips overlapping horizontally, held in place by criss-cross strips vertically and marked the position of the plasters by tracing round them with indelible pencil. The cabinet was then closed and the light in the seance room left burning. A shorthand record was taken of what followed and here it is:

The Rev. Drayton Thomas gave the invocation. There was a little music and within a few minutes a voice said, 'Good evening.' This voice was very loud and clear. Mr Drayton Thomas replied, 'Very glad to hear your voice!'
ANOTHER VOICE: Hello, can you hear?
ANSWER: Yes, we can hear you quite well.
MICKEY: Hello, Dray!
DRAYTON THOMAS: Hello, Mickey, delighted to hear you especially under these difficult conditions!
A SITTER: Is Leslie all right? Is he comfortable, Mickey?
(No reply)
VOICE: Hello, can you hear me?
ANSWER: Yes, we can hear you, friend, quite well.
(Mr Flint's breathing became very heavy.)
VOICE: Yes, I think so – wonder if they would like to have —
MICKEY: Hello, how are you? Dray, how are you?
DRAYTON THOMAS: Cheered by hearing you, Mickey, try and see how loud you can shout in these difficult conditions.

VOICE: All in good time! (There were two voices in discussion, talking quite quietly, and not every word was clear enough to be heard, but one voice said, 'Yes, we must do that, yes, I know, we will do that. He is all right now.')

SITTER: We cannot hear so well, can you speak a little louder?

VOICE: There is a certain tenseness there. We have to make allowances. Would you like to have a look at the medium?

DRAYTON THOMAS: You know we have full light here?

VOICE: Just to satisfy yourselves.

DR WEST: Do you mean we may look at the medium now? We are ready to raise the curtain if you are ready for us. We are willing to look now if you say so!

VOICE: Go ahead.

Dr West then raised the curtain. Mr Flint was in his chair in trance, with straps and adhesive tape intact. Dr West made a close inspection and then closed the curtain. (This was at 8.15 p.m.)

VOICE: Quite all right?

DR WEST: Thank you, friend.

DRAYTON THOMAS: You seem to have him in very deep trance!

VOICE: Very necessary for such an experiment.

DRAYTON THOMAS: Willis! Music, please!

VOICE: Don't be impatient, Mr Drayton Thomas!

DRAYTON THOMAS: I suppose I am impatient just now, but for this I have really a lot of patience and staying power.

VOICE: How long have you been in this now?

DRAYTON THOMAS: Thirty years!

VOICE: How is your wife?

DRAYTON THOMAS: Thank you, she is very well, better than she has been for a very long time.

VOICE: I am very glad. I want you to realise we are working here under great difficulties.

DRAYTON THOMAS: That is obvious, but we are getting so many voices!

MICKEY: What about me? I'm here, you know.

DRAYTON THOMAS: Yes, Mickey, we are very glad to hear you so clearly.

VOICE: (*very loud and clear*) God bless you all. This is White Wing. I am very pleased to be here. I want you to realise we are working under difficulties but we are very happy to be here with you.

ANSWER: Thank you very much, we are very glad to hear you.

WHITE WING: You know, Mr Willis, your cabinet is not dark, no! The light comes in through the top – not through the vent, through the curtain. It makes it more difficult. Never mind, we are very anxious to help you and co-operate with you all.

DR WEST: We are very pleased to hear that.

WHITE WING: I want you to know we do all in our power to help you, and we wanted you to see your medium half-way through your sitting. Do you realise it did not affect the medium? We want you to know we have many experiments we want to make with you, and want to show you so much, but be patient, do not lose heart. All of us here on the other side send you our love and greetings until we meet again. Farewell!

The curtain was raised slowly. Mr Flint was still in trance. Dr West again examined the strappings and adhesive tape, then removed the tape. Mr Flint said he had not been aware that the curtain was raised during the sitting. On behalf of the four guests present Dr West expressed appreciation at having been allowed to witness such an extremely interesting demonstration and particularly to thank Mr Flint for his arduous part in making the experiment possible.

Although I had been in trance throughout the test sitting which had saved me from experiencing the actual discomfort of the straps binding me to my chair or of the plasters sealing my mouth so tightly I could hardly breathe, when I came to myself after the seance I was absolutely exhausted. This exhaustion persisted even after a night's rest and so, knowing my sitters were unlikely to get results while I was in this depleted state, I cancelled all my appointments for some days to give myself a chance to recover my normal vitality. To say the least I was chagrined to hear from Drayton Thomas that one of the psychical researchers present at the test had decided I could speak from my stomach! A few days later I received a letter from Dr West to say he was not satisfied with the test sitting because at the end of it he had observed that one of the plasters sealing my lips was no longer in line with the indelible pencil marking. He accepted blame for not taking sufficient care in applying the plaster but said that since it had moved the test was spoiled and without value. He asked me to submit to a further test at the premises of the Society for Psychical Research under conditions of his own devising and offered to pay a fee for my services if I did so. I am afraid I was disappointed enough and hurt enough to refuse to consider this invitation.

My temperament is mercurial and an unexpected treat can lift me from the depths of depression to the peaks of happiness so when I found a letter from Mae West on my breakfast table which asked me to give her a sitting all my misery and resentment over what I felt, probably quite wrongly, to be the unfairness of the psychical researchers vanished and I was sitting on Cloud Nine. At that time Mae West was appearing in her own Broadway success *Diamond Lil* at the Prince of Wales Theatre in London and it was arranged I would give her a sitting in her suite at the Savoy Hotel after her evening performance.

A man introducing himself as Miss Mae West's manager and who I later learned was Mr Timoney met me when I arrived at the Savoy Hotel and conducted me to Mae's suite which was as grand and luxurious as you would expect a star to have. I was hardly surprised to see several well-tailored men sitting around among the many floral tributes and gift-wrapped packages which littered the drawing-room of the suite. Mr Timoney gave a casual wave in their general direction and muttered something about show business and I never did get any of them sorted out into individuality.

When Mae West herself entered, the standardised luxury of the hotel apartment at once took on life, personality and glamour. She was in her fifties at this time but I found it hard to believe she was not a girl. She was dazzlingly attractive and her complexion was truly lovely. I was surprised to find how tiny she was because I had always imagined she was tall and statuesque. She came over to sit beside me and we talked about her films all of which I had seen and enjoyed. Shortly Mr Timoney shepherded the anonymous show business gentlemen out of the apartment and I was alone with her. Anti-climactic it may be but we went on talking and soon we were discussing psychic matters. I learned Mae West was very far from the blatant sex symbol she represented on stage and screen. She neither smoked nor drank and her moral standards were more stringent than most; her conversation was both witty and highly intelligent and she had spent years reading widely in the fields of psychic research and comparative religion before finding her own truth in Spiritualism and then through meditation and self-discipline developing psychic power of her own. She was and still is a most remarkable woman and I count it a privilege to be one of her friends.

During our seance various entities spoke to Mae before her mother came, referring to herself as Matilda. Mae and her mother talked affectionately together for some time then Mae doubtless as a test asked her mother to mention the special pet name Mae had given to her in her lifetime. The mother answered 'Diamond Tilly'. Later, Mae told me she had called her mother by this somewhat extraordinary name because after the success of each of her Broadway shows Mae had invariably presented her mother with a brooch, a ring or earrings in diamonds. Mae's mother also told her on request that her name before marriage to Mae's father had been Doelger.

After this sitting at the Savoy Hotel Mae came on several occasions to sit with me in my house at Hendon. No one could possibly mistake Mae for anything but a great star and her arrival created a sensation each time she came.

A spirit who quoted word for word a verse on her own memorial card was a highspot of another of my demonstrations in the Kingsway Hall. The spirit voice of a woman said her name was Beatrice May Strude and she wanted to speak to Laura. A woman in the crowded hall called out to say she was Laura. 'It's me, it's Beatie!' said the spirit voice, 'Oh, I'm so glad I can speak to you.'

'Speak up and tell me something, Beat,' called Laura. 'I'm doing my best,' answered the spirit, 'I died on 6 February 1945 and I was fifty-seven, or was I fifty-eight?' 'Where did you come from?' asked Laura and was answered at once, 'New Zealand.' Then Laura was herself questioned by the spirit voice. 'Are you going back to New Zealand?' Laura said she intended to return. 'Did you go down to Bedford? That was where we were together last,' said Beatrice, 'I remember the verse you wrote on my memorial card.' Later we learned Beatrice and Laura were cousins and dear friends and it was in Bedford that Beatrice's body was buried.

'Can you tell me the words on the card, Beat?' asked Laura. 'I'll try,' responded the spirit voice, then very slowly recited nine lines of a sentimental verse word for word. 'That's right, Beat,' said Laura. 'I know you are going back to New Zealand in a fortnight,' continued the irrepressible Beatrice, adding, 'Do you remember Hetty Court?' Laura said she did and Beatrice told her Hetty was now in the spirit world and 'she had to change a few of her ideas. You know she was a Christian Scientist?' Beatrice suddenly announced: 'Spurgeon is here!' Whereupon Laura stood up and informed the audience that she and her cousin Beatrice Strude were direct descendants of the famous preacher.

When Edith was again able to lead a normal even if a sadly restricted life and the household was running smoothly under Bill's management, my Committee sent me further and further afield to demonstrate in as many provincial towns and cities as possible. I would leave London on the day of the demonstration accompanied by Father Sharp or Drayton Thomas or whoever was to act as chairman at my meeting and when we reached our destination we would stay in each other's company all the time until the demonstration so that the chairman could honestly assure the audience the medium had had no opportunity to glean information by looking round cemeteries, studying directories, listening to local gossip or by any other means. After the meeting I would travel back to London. These out-of-town meetings were especially tiring because of the double journey and the unfamiliar conditions, but I never begrudged the effort they cost me because many thousands who might otherwise never have had the opportunity experienced the most comforting of all contacts with their dead through the direct voice.

I remember an occasion at the Central Salem Hall in Leeds when one of the most evidential communications of the meeting made the audience of twelve hundred people rock with laughter. Mickey spoke to a woman sitting in the front of the hall and asked her if she let rooms to 'theatricals'. When the lady admitted she did, Mickey told her there was a 'bloke' who wanted to speak to her who had played the cat in Dick Whittington seven or eight years before, adding: 'He was so small he seemed like a dwarf.' The woman started to say she thought she knew who it was when she was interrupted by the spirit himself speaking excitedly. 'This is a rum do, isn't it?' he said, 'I never thought I'd ever speak to you like this! Do you remember when I was in Dick Whittington at the Theatre Royal?' 'Of course I do,' replied the lady, 'do you still like fish and chips?' This brought a reminder from Mickey that such things were not needed in the spirit world. Dick Whittington's cat chipped in again to say: 'I was the best cat in the business, there wasn't anyone to touch me.' His friend in the audience replied, '*I* always thought you were.' Dick's cat then reminded the lady of a photograph of himself in her possession which showed him in his cat's costume, holding the head in his hands, and asked her if she still had the bed with the brass knobs. The lady, who was later identified as Miss Hennessey of Brunswick Terrace, Leeds, said she had disposed of it. Mickey then spoke to her again to tell her that the Cat was now talking about Bella and saying 'she was letting it rip now!' When Miss Hennessey informed the audience that Bella was the Cat's wife, the hall rocked with laughter.

A psychical researcher whose name I have long since forgotten once propounded in print a theory that the voices my sitters hear are not real voices but through a combination of hypnotic power on my part and subconscious longing on the part of my sitters auditory hallucinations are induced which appear to say what the sitter longs to hear. This glib little theory was smartly knocked on the head when in September 1948 during a demonstration at Denison House, London, S.W.1, an American wire recording apparatus was used in order to produce gramophone records of the spirit voices. This experiment was highly successful, every message was recorded as clearly as when it was first spoken by the discarnate communicator. I hoped for a long time that the father of the auditory hallucination theory would explain how it was possible to record delusionary voices, but as far as I know he never did.

In his capacity as a member of the Council of the S.P.R. Drayton Thomas had made contact with another psychical researcher who was an electronics expert and able to provide various devices which could be used to prove or to disprove the reality of my voices and a series of tests were held, some at the flat of the electronics expert, others on the premises of the

Society for Psychical Research under the aegis of the Rev. Drayton Thomas and in the presence of such notable researchers as Brigadier R. C. Firebrace, c.b.e., Father Arthur Sharp, Mr F. Sibley and others too numerous to mention here.

The conditions under which I sat for these tests were: (a) my lips were sealed with plaster, (b) a throat microphone was attached to my throat and wired to amplifiers so that the slightest sound made through my own larynx would be magnified enormously, (c) the researchers were able to watch my every movement in the dark by means of an infra-red telescope and finally, (d) my hands were held by a sitter on either side of me.

Voices spoke at many of the tests under these conditions and on more than one occasion a researcher viewing through the infra-red telescope was able to see the ectoplasmic larynx through which the discarnate speak forming on my left side some two feet distant from me which is the point in space where the spirit voices are normally located during my seances.

My thanks are due to Brigadier Firebrace for his courtesy in allowing me to quote an extract from his recent letter to me which speaks for itself:

I well remember the test sittings I had with you and Drayton Thomas. At these sittings, during the seance we had an infra-red telescope focused on you and you had a throat microphone round your throat. There was an electronic expert present who watched the instruments which were attached to the throat microphone. I can well remember that under these conditions we got the direct voice without any indication on the instruments that it was registered by the throat microphone. But the voices were fainter than on previous sittings I had had with you. An interesting point was on the final occasion when with a voice speaking faintly the infra-red telescope suddenly fused; the voice

168

immediately doubled in volume. This indicated to me that infra-red rays weaken mediumship in some way. I must add you could not possibly have known that the infra-red telescope was out of action. Altogether an impressive exhibition of mediumistic power.

I think I can safely say I am the most tested medium this country has ever produced and, I will add, the medium most willing to be tested whenever I have felt truth would be served by submitting to conditions imposed on me by those I believed to be genuine researchers. I have been boxed up, tied up, sealed up, gagged, bound and held and still the voices have come to speak their message of life eternal. I have given sittings extempore in hotel rooms, in the houses of strangers, in foreign countries, in halls, theatres and churches, often under conditions where it has been impossible to obtain complete darkness or when the mental climate has been that of extreme scepticism or even downright hostility and still the voices have come.

When first I began to allow myself to be tested I was naïve enough to believe that if the tests were successful the scientists and researchers who had carried them out under their own conditions would proclaim to the world the truth of life after death. All too soon I learned the hard way that many of those who call themselves researchers have immutable values of their own which preclude belief in a meaning or purpose in man's existence or in the possibility of a life after death. Their concern was rather to disprove the reality of my voices and they would postulate any alternative however far-fetched or absurd sooner than admit the implication of their own successful experiment. I was therefore doubly blessed when I met and was tested by men of the calibre of the Rev. Drayton Thomas, Father Arthur Sharp and Brigadier Firebrace who, when the tests they made were successful, publicly stated their conviction.

A favourite explanation of my voice phenomena is that I

am some kind of super-ventriloquist-cum-mimic. I fear those who seriously entertain this absurd theory display complete ignorance of the art of ventriloquism. Any ventriloquist will tell you it is impossible for him to work in complete darkness. He needs a dummy or puppet with movable jaws to help to create his illusion and to distract the attention of his audience from the slight movements of his own facial muscles, inevitable because he is using his own voice. As to my supposed talent for mimicry, when I tell you that literally thousands of different voices of discarnate persons have been tape-recorded for posterity, speaking in different dialects, in foreign languages unknown to me and even in languages no longer spoken on this earth I think you must agree that mimicry as a theory does not hold even one small drop of water.

When all other theories have been found to be untenable your cast-iron sceptic does not hesitate to postulate downright fraud to explain the phenomena of the voices. It has been hinted that I might have a two-way voice channel to another room where accomplices mimic the voices of the departed or that I might conceal tape-recorders which play previously prepared messages from the dead. There is no end to the ingenious tricks which have been thought up by those determined not to believe and who more often than not have never even had a sitting with me. If I were to pay any attention to the nonsense talked by such silly and obdurate persons I might with justice ask them how these hidden mimics or concealed tape-recorders can hold long two-way conversations with sitters in which a mass of personal detail and reminiscence on the part of the discarnate entity builds up irrefutable evidence of his or her continued existence. I could also ask these stubborn cynics how these supposed accomplices of mine however skilled their mimicry contrive to reproduce the recognisable voice of a wife or a husband or other dead relative of a sitter who is as likely as not newly arrived from Australia, India or Timbuctoo. I do not however waste my time or my precious energies bandying words with sceptics who are as ill-informed as they are prejudiced. I and the many thousands who have sat with me know the truth.

When War broke out and I turned down the kind offer of refuge in America for the duration of hostilities I imagine my feelings as I did so were akin to those of Caesar refusing the Crown of Rome because since I was a filmstruck and starstruck small boy there was no country I longed more ardently to visit. And so I was overjoyed when in the summer of 1949 I was given another chance to visit the States and after the initial cold douche when I discovered that £5 sterling was the total amount I would be permitted to take with me, and the flurry of getting visas, guarantors and medical certificates was over I settled Edith in her daughter's house in St Albans and sailed for New York.

Twelve

THE *Queen Mary* was still beautiful but years of wartime trooping had left her shabby and down-at-heel, a tired and ageing lady badly in need of a face-lift. We were three in a small cabin and I did not need to be a psychic to sense the hatred between the two other men. One was a German, the other a Polish Jew, and neither spoke the language of the other nor English. Non-communication in that cabin was total except for the implacable loathing which filled it like a live and malevolent thing. During the five days of the voyage I wondered what personal tragedy each man might have left behind him in the post-war chaos of his country which could have bred such malignance.

One morning after we had been at sea for a couple of days a steward knocked and entered the cabin before I had had time to escape from the oppressive miasma surrounding my room-mates into the fresh air on deck. 'The Captain presents his compliments to you, Mr Flint,' began the steward politely, 'he wonders if you would be good enough to take a Holy Communion Service on Sunday at eleven?' The notion that such an august personage as the Captain should know I even existed was dumbfounding enough, let alone his curious request, and I suppose I stood, stupid and open-mouthed, trying to work it out. 'You are down on the passenger list as a Minister of Religion,' said the steward with a patient sigh, 'will you take the service?' 'Of course not!' I blurted out. 'I'm not that kind of minister at all!' The steward heaved a bigger and even more patient sigh and left, clearly wondering what kind of a nut I was. I wondered why I had listened to Father Sharp when he had instructed me how to fill in my application for my first passport.

On the morning of our fifth day at sea we sailed into American waters and there ahead of us was the Statue of Liberty and the thrilling skyline of New York.

In the Customs shed sudden panic hit me. Suppose the friends who had invited me to America failed to meet me? I had no money except for the paltry remains of my £5 and no prospect of earning any. I would be stranded in a strange country without even the price of a bed that night. The cavalier treatment meted out by the customs official did nothing to reassure me. By way of searching for contraband he simply turned my neatly packed case upside-down so that its contents fell on the ground, rummaged through, then left me to repack. When he was finished with me I was already in imagination haggard, unkempt and panhandling for dimes on Skid Row. As soon as I emerged from the Customs shed the warmth of my friends' welcome banished the hungry panhandler to the hinterlands of my consciousness.

When I saw the apartment my friends had taken for me my heart sank. This temporary home of mine consisted of an entire floor of one of the old brownstone houses in West 88th Street, once one of the smart residential districts of New York but at that time fallen on less palmy days. The furnishings of the apartment seemed to me the epitome of sybaritic comfort and the bathroom was the biggest and most luxurious I had ever seen in my life. I immediately began to fret about how I was going to pay for it all; but before I gave myself an ulcer I learned I was the guest of the Rev. Mrs Bertha Marx, a noted medium who was the head of the W. T. Stead Centre, the Spiritualist Society which occupied the ground floor of the brownstone house and was so named in memory of W. T. Stead, editor, reformer and Spiritualist who was lost at sea in the disaster of the *Titanic*. Dear Bertha Marx! She not only provided me with a roof over my head, she organised my work and introduced me to many of the best-known Spiritualists in America and in every way in her power she made my stay in New York a happy and memorable one.

I also made a new and delightful friend in Caroline Chapman, 'Chappie', who was and still is one of the most loved mediums in America as well as one of the few whose psychic gifts have been endorsed by the American Society for Psychical Research, which is just as tough and just as sceptical as its British counterpart.

I loved New York and I spent many hours just walking in its streets, discovering it, getting the feel of it. Sometimes I got lost in its great confusion and it took me a while to master the subway sufficiently to get on a train going in the right direction, but even getting lost was fun in that city of infinite variety.

The most impressive spirit communication is that in which information is given by a discarnate person which is not only unknown to anyone present but is even rejected as untrue, yet which subsequent inquiry proves to be correct. Such a communication rules out the overworked theory of telepathy and can be regarded not merely as evidence of survival but as cast-iron proof.

Such a communication was given at a group for seventy-five persons which I held at the W. T. Stead Centre and the American recipient of it was Mr Robert F. Bolton, then living at 40 East 49th Street, New York City.

After various spirits had spoken to their friends, Mickey announced the presence of one who was known on earth as Carl Schneider. No one in the room responded, no one apparently knew him. Mickey persisted, declaring someone in the room knew Carl Schneider and that person must speak up to help him communicate. 'I know a man of that name,' said Mr Bolton, at last, 'but to the best of my knowledge he is alive and well.' Nothing daunted, Mickey asserted Carl Schneider was on the other side and he was about to speak. Carl's voice was then heard and he and Mr Bolton conversed. 'When did you pass away?' inquired Mr Bolton. 'About twelve months ago, maybe a little over a year,' the spirit replied. 'It was Carl's voice! I recognised its unmistakable husky quality,' declared Mr Bolton after the seance.

Mr Bolton found the return of his friend Carl Schneider so totally unexpected he was in a state of agitation until he could confirm whether his friend was alive or dead. On the morning after the seance the first thing he did was to call a telephone number Carl had once given him. When the phone was answered he asked to speak to Carl Schneider and the answer came: 'I am sorry, but Carl passed away.' Because he still could not believe it, Mr Bolton then asked: 'Are you sure?' The voice at the other end of the line replied: 'I ought to be. I am the one who found him. He committed suicide about a year ago.'

Robert Bolton returned to sit in another group of mine and on this occasion Mickey singled him out to tell him Carl was glad he had 'checked up' because now he would know the truth of survival.

I have taken my account of Mr Bolton's experience from a letter which Mr Bolton wrote, completely unsolicited, to *Psychic News* in London describing what happened at my group seance. In his letter, Mr Bolton, in assessing the value of his experience, comments: 'I am not so naïve as to believe this account will cause belief in the spirit world to come as a revelation to a scoffing sceptic. This report however may inspire some honest sceptic to expose himself to the possibility of such an experience. It is the only scientific approach to truth....'

Too soon I had to leave New York for Chicago where a big public demonstration had been organised for me in the Kimball Hall. When I sallied forth from my hotel on my first evening there to take a look at the city almost the first thing I saw was Bea Lillie's name in lights over the entrance to a theatre. She was starring with Ray Bolger in *Hey! Hey!*

U.S.A.! and I went in to see the show. I enjoyed it enormously and Bea and Ray together made me laugh so much it hurt. I went round after the performance and found Bea the same charming and friendly person as ever in spite of her fabulous success in the States and all the adulation it had brought her.

When I turned up at the Kimball Hall the following evening to give my demonstration I was met with a bombshell. My sponsors had arranged to borrow a cabinet for me from another medium but the medium had left town and the cabinet was locked in his apartment and no one had the keys. Furthermore, it was impossible to darken the hall and every ticket had been sold, every seat was filled, they were standing in the aisles. 'Give them a lecture and follow it with clairvoyance,' said one of my sponsors with what I thought was maddening insouciance. I told him it was years since I had given clairvoyance in public. Without a word this incurable optimist indicated the serried ranks of the audience waiting for 'the famous London medium' to appear. Even if I were to give a lecture followed by clairvoyance, what would be the reaction of an audience who had paid for a demonstration of direct voice? My sanguine friend thought they would understand when we explained it to them, and to my amazement, they did. When I walked on to the platform, I was greeted by warm-hearted applause. Almost at once thoughts and impressions came flooding into my mind and I started to speak. I finished my lecture to applause and, my self-confidence restored and the butterflies in my stomach at rest, I began my clairvoyance. If I may use the word in this context it was a bravura performance. For one solid hour evidence simply poured out of me. Not one name went unrecognised, not one message was unclaimed. Apart from the pleasure of giving happiness to the recipients it was sheer joy for me to find this facet of my mediumship was still able to function so well. When I left my hotel the next morning to go sightseeing I was surprised to be stopped in the streets by complete strangers who wanted to thank me for evidence they had been given or who pleaded with me to sit for them privately. I had to disappoint all of them because it was time I went on my way to Los Angeles to be the guest of Dr Carl Menugh in his Long Beach apartment where I had agreed to hold seances for a few of his friends.

My only contact with Dr Menugh had been by correspondence, so when I arrived at Los Angeles station I looked about me for a cosy family doctor kind of man who might be my host. I saw no one who answered this description so I stood around trying to look like 'the famous medium from London' by gazing aloofly into the middle distance while wishing fervently I had worn a quieter tie. Shortly I was greeted by a man no older than myself who was Carl Menugh, his doctorate I later learned was in philosophy.

Perhaps the most dramatic seance I held in Los Angeles was one at which a father returned to tell his son the truth about his death and to exonerate the driver of the vehicle which killed him.

The son whom I shall call Bill was brought with his wife to a group seance by their friend Miss Artie Blackburn of Los Angeles. All Miss Blackburn told me about the friends she wished to bring to sit in my group was that the husband was a brilliant inventor and scientist who would subject any evidence he might receive to analysis and would refuse to accept anything which could not be proved.

At the sitting Mickey spoke to Bill and asked if he was associated with the Texaco Corporation. Bill answered that he was but he supposed Miss Blackburn had given this information to the medium. This, both Mickey and Miss Blackburn stoutly denied, and in point of fact I never allow friends of sitters to give me any information about them because not only would it render any evidence which may come valueless but I have found when someone inadvertently gives me information before a sitting it makes me so self-conscious that the sitting is just as likely to be a blank. 'Was your father killed very suddenly in an accident?' was Mickey's next question to Bill, who said this was correct. 'What is La Brea?' asked Mickey next. 'It is the name of the bus which killed my father,' was Bill's reply. (It is the practice of some passenger vehicle operators in the States to name their rolling stock.) 'Your Dad says it wasn't the driver's fault as you all thought, and he says you sued the Company which was too bad because it was all his own fault. He thought he was spry enough to get across ahead of the bus. He says the driver hadn't a chance, it wasn't his fault at all.' Mickey, prompted by the voice of Bill's father, went on to describe the exact circumstances of the accident, then suddenly changed the subject: 'Your Dad is saying you did not do what he wanted with his Masonic watch and chain.' Bill, rather hurt, replied that he had given it to a friend of his father's, thinking that was what his father wished. 'You gave him the watch,' said Mickey, 'but what about the chain?' Bill's wife chipped in here, 'Oh, dear,' she said, 'I kept the chain, I wanted to wear it myself.' The next message Mickey relayed from Bill's father asked him not to visit the cemetery so often. 'Your Dad says you take flowers from his own garden to put on his grave and he would rather see them growing than on a grave where he is not.' It was true that Bill took flowers to the grave from his father's garden because Bill and his wife were now living in the father's former home. 'What about your Dad's stick?' asked Mickey next. 'My father never walked with a stick in his life,' answered Bill. Undaunted, Mickey replied, 'He's talking about the stick he kept in the chest. He went round with it at night rapping on doors and locks to see everything was fastened up tight.' 'Oh, that stick!' said Bill, 'it's still in the chest.'

When Bill was asked later what he thought of the sitting, he said: 'This is the most wonderful night of my life. This is the night my spiritual unfoldment begins.'

On a subsequent evening Bill had another sitting with me and on that occasion his father spoke to him and his wife in a voice which Bill recognised as his father's own.

I had got used to the way the warm-hearted Americans telephoned complete strangers like myself to offer hospitality so I was not unduly surprised when a Mr Le Fevre suggested driving me to Hollywood to spend the day with his wife and himself. Hollywood! The very name of it uttered casually on the telephone by a stranger was enough to thrill me with memories of past enchantments. In spite of the years which had passed, at heart I was still the star-struck boy in the fourpennies.

As we drove along Sunset Boulevard and began the climb into Beverly Hills, Mr Le Fevre told me he and his wife had recently sold their chain of hotels in San Francisco and bought their Hollywood home for their retirement. 'It once belonged to Rudolph Valentino, the film star,' said my new friend. 'Did you ever hear of him?' Down the years echoed the voice of Valentino, 'One day when he is a famous medium he will hold a seance in the room which was my bedroom in my house in Hollywood and I will come to speak to him there.' Then I saw the sign by the road which said 'Falcon Lair' and the car turned off to the house.

It was a charming house and Mr and Mrs Le Fevre were the kindest of hosts, so when they asked me to hold seances for them and a few of their friends I was happy to agree. When they asked me to choose a room in which to hold the seances I said I thought the room opening off the patio would be most suitable and it surprised me not at all when Mr Le Fevre remarked, 'That room was Valentino's bedroom.'

Valentino came through at the first seance I held in 'Falcon Lair' and almost the first thing he said after greeting us was how happy it made him to be able to fulfil the promise he had made to me so many years before. He thanked Mr and Mrs Le Fevre for inviting me and told them he was glad they were happy in his old home, but he was afraid they would be selling it again before long. This brought a gasp from Mr Le Fevre since he had acquired the house only a few months pre-

179

viously and intended to make it the headquarters of a World Peace movement. Valentino must have sensed Mr Le Fevre's uneasiness because he hastened to assure him there was no unpleasantness impending. The Le Fevres would continue their work for World Peace in the house for a short time then they would prefer to live elsewhere and they would sell 'Falcon Lair'.

After the seance we sat in the big drawing-room of the house with the curtains open so we could see the whole of Hollywood spread out before us, a glitter of lights romantic and beautiful in the distance. I found it hard to believe I was really sitting in Rudolph Valentino's drawing-room looking out over the film city just as he must have done so many times in his lifetime. As I sat marvelling, suddenly I knew with certainty that Valentino had never been happy in this house nor would anyone else ever be happy in it. Months later when I was in London someone sent me a cutting from a Los Angeles paper which said the Le Fevres had sold 'Falcon Lair' to Doris Duke the tobacco heiress and had moved elsewhere.

I made another vicarious contact with Valentino when I met Mae Murray. In the days of silent films Mae was M.G.M.'s most glamorous star, the uncrowned queen of Hollywood. Her blonde curls, bee-stung mouth and lithe dancer's figure fascinated the Jazz Age generation and brought her riches, fame and adulation, but the coming of sound pictures and a disastrous marriage to Prince David Mdivani toppled her from her throne and when I met her she was living in circumstances sadly reduced from the days when her Rolls-Royce had solid gold and cloisonne fittings and lap rugs of sable. Mae was still vividly attractive and she was a joy to be with because of her delicious sense of humour and a complete lack of self-pity, though few women have been so dishonestly exploited as Mae was in the days when her name on any picture rang chimes at the box office.

Mae and her first husband, Bob Leonard the director, gave Valentino his first chance as a leading man in films when he was an unknown dancer on the fringes of the film industry and there had grown up between Mae and Valentino a true and deep friendship which endured until his untimely death. Talking to Mae, listening to her stories about Valentino, I came more and more to know and admire the good and gentle person behind the studio image of Great Lover.

Mae West entertained me in her Hollywood home, which was in a huge block of luxury apartments known as the Ravenswood Apartments. Mae not only lived in it, she owned the whole block, for unlike many big stars she is an excellent business woman and over the years she has invested her enormous earnings wisely and well. I found the decor of her home startling to say the least of it. It was almost entirely white. Walls, carpets, curtains, furniture, everything was white with here and there occasional splashes of dramatic colour, a spray of scarlet flowers in a white bowl, a jade cushion on a white settee. The whole seemed designed to highlight and dramatise a lifesize statue of Mae in the nude which dominated the room. As a setting for Mae's blonde good looks and vivid personality it was superb, but I could not help feeling homesick for Edith and the shabbiness of Sydney Grove.

The day before I left Hollywood was the anniversary of Valentino's death so I made a sentimental journey to the Memorial Cemetery to put some flowers on his grave. I found his white marble mausoleum already heaped with blooms and a cemetery attendant told me that even though it was twenty years and more since his death, these tributes from all over the world had been arriving at the cemetery all day. The same attendant pointed out a vase in the crypt which held thirteen roses, twelve red, one white, and told me I had just missed seeing the Lady in Black, the mystery woman in deep mourning who appeared at the tomb with the thirteen roses on each anniversary of the star's death.

Some years after my near-encounter with the Lady in Black she herself revealed the story behind her annual pilgrimage to the Memorial Cemetery and because it throws lights on a side of Valentino's nature with which the public who adored his romantic image was not familiar I will retell the story here. The Lady in Black was a violinist and pianist, her name was Ditra Flame. She had met Valentino in 1918 when he was poor and unknown, trying to make a career as a dancer. Ditra was then fourteen years old; soon after their meeting she became gravely ill and was sent to hospital. The child was frightened she would die and obsessed by the idea that no one would care, or remember her when she was dead. Valentino spent hours at her bedside, trying to give her the will to live and comforting her. Each time he came to see her he brought her red roses which at that point in his career he must have ill afforded. One day when he found her crying and insisting that death was near and she would be lonely and forgotten in her grave, Valentino promised that if she were to die he would bring red roses to her grave every day. 'But remember,' he added, 'if I die first I don't want to be lonely or forgotten either.' He did die first and Ditra did not forget.

Although letters from home had been unfailingly cheerful I began to feel uneasy about Edith's health, and as soon as I reached New York I booked my passage home on the *Queen Mary*.

When I walked into our sitting-room in Sydney Grove the way Edith's face lit up when she saw me was reward enough for cutting short my stay in America. She was sitting in a chair by the open window, and since it was a warm summer's day I wondered why she had a rug draped over her knees. When I knelt by her side to hold her hands and ask her all the questions crowding into my mind I discovered the reason for the rug, Edith was hoping to conceal from me as long as possible the fact that she was in a wheelchair. When Edith saw my face she knew, as she always did know, what was in my mind and she smiled, almost the old radiant smile. 'I love my chair, darling,' she said, 'I can get about so marvellously, into the garden, everywhere.'

Later that night I slipped round to see Edith's doctor and asked him to tell me the truth about my wife's health. He told me Edith had suffered another minor stroke during my absence and it was unlikely she would ever walk again. When I asked the inevitable question he gave it as his opinion that my wife would not live longer than two years at most. I determined they would be two of the happiest of her life.

While I had been away my Committee had organised a heavy schedule for me; there were big meetings arranged in London, Birmingham, Leeds, Liverpool and many other towns and cities, and these were nearly always held in halls or theatres holding up to two thousand people. I have never owned a car but whenever it was possible to get a train home after these meetings I would dash to the station for it, however late. When I got home I would make a pot of tea and take a tray up to our bedroom and Edith and I would drink tea together while I told her everything, the evidence which had come through at the meeting, the amusing little happenings before it. I would look forward all day in whatever strange town or city I happened to be to these late night talks.

Bill's affection for Edith was expressed in the efforts he made to contrive imaginative and tasty meals to tempt her appetite and by his constant care for her comfort. I would sometimes make arrangements with the manager of the local cinema and Bill and I would take Edith in her wheelchair to see a film. She loved these outings, they made her feel part of ordinary life and cheered her enormously.

At one of my meetings in the Kingsway Hall a spirit who had an urgent desire to communicate with his parents found a way to do so even though his parents were not among the two thousand people in the hall. A number of messages had been relayed when Mickey spoke of the presence of a young man who refused to give his name but who described how he had taken his own life while his parents were at the Empire Theatre in Hackney, 'It was done in a mad moment, I regret it now. They came back from the Empire and found me hanging from the banisters.' Immediately a Mr Shead sitting in the auditorium remembered meeting a man at a social gathering a few weeks before who had told him of his son's inexplicable suicide which had occurred in the circumstances described by the spirit communicator. 'I know about that boy!' Mr Shead called out, adding: 'I met his father recently and he told me about his son's tragic death!' Mickey returned to speak to Mr Shead. 'The boy is desperately anxious for his parents to know he is alive and that he is sorry for causing them such grief. Will you tell them so?' Mr Shead promised he would.

At this same meeting another suicide manifested to express regret for what he had done. Mrs Bullock of Kenton was greeted by the voice of her husband and he spoke of being accompanied by a young man whose name he gave. Mickey chipped in to fill in details: 'The young man was in the Home Guard and he wants you to tell his mother how sorry he is for what he did. He knows what a terrible shock she got when she found him in the kitchen. Please give his love to Pearl.' Mrs Bullock then told the audience the young man had lived in her village and he had shot himself in the kitchen of his parents' home. Pearl was his girl friend.

Not all my meetings went smoothly, I remember one at the Corn Exchange in Bedford where Mickey accepted a challenge from a persistent interrupter who alleged there was a hidden microphone in the hall through which an accomplice was playing the part of Mickey. Mickey had singled out a Mrs Bonning and introduced a spirit communicator called Punter whom he said Mrs Bonning knew. She agreed she had known Mr Punter whereupon the spirit himself spoke to her. In a clear strong voice he said he came from Luton where he had owned a hat factory. 'We had a fire and I tried to save some of the girls who were trapped,' he said. Mrs Bonning recalled the fire and added, 'You were attached to the Luton Spiritualist Church.' 'No,' replied the spirit, 'that was my brother.' The discarnate Mr Punter was still speaking when a young Air

Force sergeant loudly demanded that the microphone be moved from in front of the cabinet. Mr Abdy Collins, who was my chairman, asked what difference this would make and the sergeant replied that for all he knew 'Mickey' might be speaking over another microphone concealed somewhere in the hall. In the midst of this altercation between Mr Collins and the sergeant Mickey himself shouted that the microphone could be moved if necessary. It was then placed a good distance away from the cabinet and to one side of it. Whereupon Mickey positively bawled, 'Can you hear me at the back of the hall?' Never before had I heard Mickey shout so loudly, his voice filled the entire hall with sound. Mr Collins asked the sergeant if he were satisfied there was no concealed microphone such as he had alleged and somewhat sheepishly the young man agreed he was, but he added truculently that he supposed the recipients of the messages to be accomplices planted among the audience. Hearing this as I sat in my cabinet I was furious at the suggestion until I remembered it was exactly what I myself had suspected of other mediums in my early days of investigation into Spiritualism. Mrs Bonning, angry at the slur on her integrity implied in the sergeant's latest accusation, stood up and replied to him with such vigour that he was silenced once and for all, but the harmony of the conditions in the hall was so disrupted by the incident that Mr Collins brought the meeting to an end.

High spots in Edith's increasingly restricted life were Owen's visits with his adorable small daughter. For days before they came she would plan with Bill what they would eat and discuss with me what small toy we might buy to surprise and delight the child. From the time they arrived until they had to go home Edith would shine with a little of the old radiance and it was almost like the old days again.

Owen's face could never hide his feelings, so one day when he came alone to see Edith I knew as soon as I saw him he had news he hated to tell. As gently as he could he told his mother that Jane's wealthy father had offered him an executive post in his business in California and he and Jane were leaving England to make a new life in America. When he had finished what he had to say, Edith said, 'Of course you must go, darling, it's a wonderful chance. I'm so happy for you.' I had never admired her more.

On the day Owen was leaving I cancelled all my work so that I could be with Edith until after the ship sailed when I felt she would need me badly. She sat patiently in her wheelchair, her hands made clumsy and uncertain by her illness, picking at a tangle of wool trying to unravel it, her eyes seldom strayed from the clock as the hour of Owen's departure grew nearer. When the clock hands closed on the hour she sighed, and again I heard myself say with the same painful inadequacy, 'I'll make a pot of tea.'

From that day Edith's health deteriorated more rapidly until the time came when she was too ill to leave her bed and the doctor warned me the end could not be far off.

One evening as I sat by her bed telling her all the doings of the day as she liked me to do I saw her face change in some indefinable way and in a small voice she said: 'I do love you so!' then she slipped into the coma which lasted for two days before her spirit was released.

The cremation was at Golders Green and the chapel was filled with our friends and bright with flowers. The organist played music Edith had loved and our old friend Father Sharp said the last farewell. There was no mourning, no tears, just the sadness of seeing a dear one off on a journey when the time of reunion is not known yet.

That night when all our friends had gone and I was alone in the room Edith and I had shared for so many years a wave of desolation swept over me as I realised I had yet to come to terms with the loss of her physical presence, the hand she would place on mine in moments of discouragement, her smile, the small private jokes we had. I wondered if I could go on living in a house filled with memories of past happiness.

Next morning there were two letters from California, one

from Owen inviting me to his home for an indefinite stay and the other from a Psychic Society in Los Angeles asking me to become their resident medium. As always when a decision touches on my spiritual work I decided to ask the advice of my unseen helpers as to which of these offers I should accept. At the next meeting of my home circle I put my question to them. To my surprise and, I must admit, my disappointment they asked me to refuse both these offers, they said I must remain in England to perform new and special work which they had in mind. They went on to tell me that the public phase of my mediumship must now cease because the big demonstrations and the journeys they made necessary, coupled with my other work, were depleting my energies to such an extent that not only my health but my mediumship itself was in danger. Finally they told me that soon a large unfurnished flat in the heart of London would be offered to me at a rent which I could afford to pay and I must accept it. I am bound to say there did not seem to be the smallest possibility of anyone offering me any such thing. There was an acute shortage of unfurnished accommodation in central London and landlords were able to charge high rents and in addition demand large sums as 'key money' from would-be tenants.

Three months later I was standing in the garden flat of a big house in Bayswater instructing the removal men where to place my furniture and wondering about the special new work I was to do in the future.

Thirteen

In all my years as a medium I have never yet disregarded advice from my helpers nor did I now ignore their warning that my gift was in danger because I had been overworking. As soon as I was settled in the new home to which, against all probability, I had been led I retired from public work. Adamantly I refused all invitations to demonstrate in the great halls throughout the country no matter how tempting the financial inducement offered. My new telephone number was not listed in the directory and I shunned publicity of any kind. I strictly limited the number of my private seances and I sat only with sincere researchers or with those whose need was great.

Obviously my income was much reduced, but the rent I paid to Leon and Rose who owned the house where I now lived was modest and I earned enough to live quietly and continue to pay Bill's wages. For the first time in my life I had time to rest, to meditate, to pursue my twin hobbies of photography and the art of the silent cinema, to enjoy the company of friends. I grew calmer, more relaxed, and my health was greatly improved.

During these months I waited to be shown the new work which those who guide me from the other side of life had told me I must do. One seance out of many, stands out in my memory because of the curious reluctance of a sceptical mother to accept or even respond to the almost frantic efforts of her deceased son to establish his identity.

Patrick Selby, Director and General Manager of an organisation which controls the activities of two leading West End theatres, came to sit with me accompanied by seven of his friends, among them was a lady whom I shall call Mrs Carr because it is not her name. As soon as the seance started it was obvious that all that transpired was directed towards trying to convince Mrs Carr that her son Justin had survived his physical death. After Mickey had greeted Mr Selby and his friends a faint voice was heard to say: 'Mother, this is Justin. It's wonderful to have this moment.' Mrs Carr, with some prompting from the other sitters, answered, but she sounded full of disbelief. With his voice never rising much above an urgent whisper Justin began trying to convince his mother of his identity by mentioning various bits of information from the past, but whatever he offered by way of evidence Mrs Carr remained aloof and disinterested. Finally, as though to clinch the matter, the dead boy asked: 'Do you remember that time on the river with the swans?' With the same cool detachment Mrs Carr replied: 'I don't believe I do.' The spirit voice took on a tinge of despair: 'But you *must* remember, Mother, the swans attacked the boat!' It seemed Mrs Carr had no recollection of this. However, a girl sitter intervened to say she remembered the incident very well, it had occurred during a time when she and her parents lived near the Carrs and the two families often went sailing together. Doubtless encouraged by this support, Justin went on reminding his mother of small happenings in his life on earth, all of which she received with the same lack of enthusiasm and palpable disbelief. At last, and one could hear exasperation in the boy's voice, he burst out with: 'Mother! I'll convince you if it kills me!' In spite of the seriousness of the occasion the other members of the group and I could not help dissolving into laughter at this statement. Sad to say, though much further evidence was given in the attempt to convince Mrs Carr of her son's survival, she left my seance room as obdurately sceptical as she had entered it.

One morning I was waiting for two friends of the Rev. Drayton Thomas for whom he had made an appointment by telephone. Like the experienced researcher Dray was, he had told me nothing about his friends apart from the fact that they were Mr and Mrs Newton. When Bill showed them into the seance room I was annoyed to see an Alsatian dog follow them in. Bill knew very well I did not allow animals in the seance room and it was on the tip of my tongue to ask him what he was thinking about when it dawned on me it was not an earthly dog.

During the seance Mr Newton's father spoke to him and after giving evidence of his identity told his son he had Rex with him, adding that at first Rex could not understand why he had been sent away from his master but now he had settled down and was quite happy 'with mother and me'. At this point to my surprise and embarrassment I heard Mr Newton sobbing.

When the seance was over I learned from Mrs Newton that the couple had recently arrived from Australia with the intention of settling in England. Before sailing Mrs Newton had persuaded her husband to have his Alsatian dog Rex put down because the move to a new country would be simpler without him. Her husband had not yet forgiven himself for acquiescing in the destruction of the dog he had loved.

This seance was not the first nor was it by any means the last at which I have heard evidence given to my sitters that some pet animal lived on in another dimension. I am convinced that the love we give to our animals on this side of life lifts them on to a higher plane of existence than that which many other forms of life achieve and that when we die we shall find them waiting to greet us.

Now and then two people on earth will make a pact that the one who dies first will make every effort to communicate from the other side and they will agree a code word or message between them which will identify the communicator and prove his survival of death. Mrs Grover, who now lives in

Dulverton, Somerset, booked a sitting with me when she lived in London some years ago with the hope that she might bring comfort to her younger daughter by making contact with the girl's husband who had recently died. At the sitting Bill, Mrs Grover's son-in-law, spoke to her calling her 'Gerry' as he did in his lifetime and asking about her health. Then in a voice fraught with strain he said: 'Mummy Bear, Daddy Bear and Brumas.' He repeated this pointless phrase many times, then said in a puzzled way: 'I don't know why I am saying this except to prove identity.' Mrs Grover was not only disappointed with her sitting, she was mystified, the phrase which had been repeated with such urgency meant nothing to her whatsoever. When she returned home and told her daughter about the nonsensical message she had been given at her sitting Bill's widow was radiantly happy. The silly phrase which Bill had uttered so often and with so great an effort was the code message the girl and her husband had agreed to try to communicate to the other should one of them die first.

Some years later Mrs Grover had another sitting with me at which Bill manifested. I do not think I can do better than to quote here an extract from Mrs Grover's own account of this sitting which she was kind enough to send to me.

We sat for several minutes and I was beginning to fear that dear Mickey would not come through, but he did and, after his usual little chat, he said: 'Bill is here, Aunty Gerry.' To my astonishment my son-in-law's first words were, 'Gerry, you are very worried about your health?' I must explain that Mr Flint had no idea I had been ill for a year before I left London with an internal complaint which was still troubling me. While I was in London on this visit I had taken the opportunity to see a surgeon and I had spent a whole day having X-rays and various tests at the London Clinic a few days previous to my sitting. The surgeon had been called to Scotland to perform an emergency operation and for this reason his secretary had told me it would be some time before he could see my X-rays. Therefore I answered Bill that I *was* rather worried about myself. Bill replied: 'There's no need for you to worry at all. I have seen your X-rays and there is no malignancy. You will not need to have an operation, surgery cannot cure a bug! But in the future you must be very careful about your diet and avoid roughage.' My son-in-law was a doctor and a specialist in radiology during his life on earth. It remains to add that on the day following this sitting the surgeon's secretary telephoned me to say that the surgeon had just seen the X-rays and she repeated almost exactly the reassuring words Bill had said to me in Mr Flint's seance room.

I had sat on many occasions with Mr S. G. Woods, a psychical researcher and a man of great integrity. Mr Woods, George, was in the habit of bringing a recording-machine to his sittings with me (paper tapes in those days) and he would play his recordings not only to members of his local Spiritualist Church but to anyone else he thought might benefit from the knowledge that man lives on after death whether he likes the idea or not. When George telephoned me one day to ask if he might bring a friend when next he sat with me I readily agreed, and when he arrived for his appointment he was accompanied by a charming lady whom he introduced as Mrs Betty Greene, explaining that this would be her first experience of the direct voice although she had listened with great interest to the recordings he had made at his seances with me. There were other sitters present when George Woods and Betty Greene sat together in my seance room for the first time and the chief communicator on this occasion was Rose Hawkins, a spirit who had spoken at other of my seances and so was sufficiently versed in the complexities of communication between the two worlds to talk fluently and intelligently in what I supposed must be a reasonably good facsimile of her earthly voice, strident, cheerful, with a Cockney twang even more pronounced than Mickey's. According to Rose's own account of herself she was a street flower seller whose pitch was near Charing Cross Station in the heart of London, and her life had been one of hardship and extreme poverty. Rose is always willing to answer questions put to her by sitters though she modestly makes it clear she has not yet advanced very far in the spiritual sense and she disclaims any knowledge of conditions in the higher planes of existence where more evolved souls dwell. When George asked Rose what it was like in her present condition of life she replied: 'Now you've asked me! You want me to describe our world in your material language! I don't know which way to start. I suppose if you could think of all the beautiful things in your world without all the things which aren't pleasant, you'd 'ave a vague notion of what it's like.'

Another sitter asked if the people in Rose's world ever thought about money and Rose was scornful. 'You can't buy anything over 'ere with money, mate! The only things you get 'ere is by character and the way you've lived your life and how you've thought and acted!'

When a member of the group wanted to know if there was law and order on the other side, Rose said: 'There's the natural law, my dear, which we all begin to recognise soon after we get 'ere. There ain't no laws and rules and regulations, like Governments 'n' that, but there are laws which are common laws and we all recognise them.'

When Rose spoke about creative work which spirits do, she was emphatic that 'they do it because they love to do it, everything here is done for love, and anyone on your side who wanted to be a musician, for instance, who never 'ad the chance in life can do all the things he wanted to do.'

As I looked back down the years I see George's invitation to Betty to sit in my group that day as the last link in a chain of events which was to lead to news of my work being spread more widely than ever before.

George and Betty sat with me privately a number of times

G

after that first occasion and they always recorded their sittings on tape so that others might share their experience. During these early years of my association with them I became more and more aware of the very special atmosphere of harmony which was created in the seance room whenever they sat together and, although in the very nature of mediumship some of their sittings were blank, at other times they would receive communication from souls who had evolved far beyond our material world.

Since the move from Hendon Bill's health had slowly worsened but because he knew death was only a step into a larger life Bill faced his terminal illness calmly, serenely, without fear. When Bram came to live with us Bill trained him in his duties he had himself performed so faithfully and then, as he wished, went back to spend what time was left to him in the town where he had passed his boyhood.

By this time George Woods and Betty Greene had been sitting with me at intervals for two or three years and one day during a sitting Ellen Terry came to speak to them and this is what she said: '*You are going to have some remarkable communications and I suggest you keep this contact regularly to build up the power and strengthen the link which has been deliberately arranged for your tapes. There are souls on this side of life with a great desire to make use of these opportunities to pass through information about life in our world and the mechanics of communication between your world and ours. The tapes you record will give us the means to reach people in your world and we shall use them to the best of our ability. We shall bring various souls from different spheres of life over here to give talks and lectures which can be sent out and played all over your world to millions of people. That is why we want you to sit regularly with this medium to build up the power and make possible the way for these various entities to come and talk to you about themselves and about many things of importance to mankind.*'

I had never doubted the reality of my voices nor questioned

the integrity of my spirit helpers, but as I listened to the familiar voice of Ellen Terry suddenly I felt miserable and uncertain. How could George's tape recordings be heard by millions of people all over the world? I knew that George during many years of psychical research had received such proof of survival that his great desire was to share his conviction with as many people as possible but – millions? It did not make sense. When Ellen Terry's voice faded I leapt from my chair to switch on the light, and asked George if he would play back his recording. When I heard Ellen Terry's extraordinary message for the second time I knew that however fantastic it might seem sooner or later George's tapes would be heard all over the world by millions of people. Then and there it was arranged that George and Betty would sit with me regularly and from that day to this they have done so.

Mrs Bryant, who lived in Palace Gate, came to sit with me from time to time and more often than not her late husband, George, would come to talk to her and give her such advice and help as was now in his power. One day Mrs Bryant arrived for an appointment accompanied by a stranger. He was a tall gaunt man whom I judged to be in his fifties and Mrs Bryant asked if he might share her sitting with her. Quite correctly Mrs Bryant did not tell me her friend's name, but by way of introduction she brightly informed me he was a complete sceptic who thought spirit communication was at best delusion and self-deception and at worst downright fraud. She added that she had persuaded him to come with her against his will in order to prove to him how wrong he was and to make him eat his words. Mrs Bryant's thumbnail sketch of my proposed new sitter's mental attitude was hardly a recommendation and as I looked at him standing in my hallway, ramrod straight with a supercilious smile, I was not drawn to him, but I was touched by Mrs Bryant's confident faith and I agreed to her request.

At the sitting Mrs Bryant's husband did not come through to greet her as he usually did, but after Mickey had spoken to both sitters for a short while a man's voice was heard to say his name was 'White' and he was glad to be able to speak to his son after such a long time. In spite of the pitch darkness I got the impression that Mrs Bryant gave her friend a sharp dig in the ribs to make him answer. He did answer but in such a bored and condescending way he would have done better to keep quiet. The spirit tried again but was met by the same lack of warmth from my reluctant sitter. A short pause ensued during which we could hear two spirit voices engaging in a whispered colloquy which from the occasional phrases I could catch sounded like a discussion on strategy. Suddenly, all three of us were jolted in our seats when the voice of the discarnate White boomed out loudly: 'I'll tell you a few things to make you sit up, son!' From then, until the end of the sitting the father poured out proofs of his identity, anecdotes of the sitter's boyhood, memories of things he and his son had done together, places they had been together, all manner of irrefutable proofs that it really was his father speaking. Before very long my sceptical sitter was animatedly keeping up his end of an intimate and evocative conversation.

When the sitting was over I must admit I was astonished when Mrs Bryant's friend stayed on after she went home and proceeded to put me through a species of third degree. I knew perfectly well who he was, didn't I? What was the name of my friend in Warwick? Mrs Bryant had phoned me early that morning, hadn't she? Where was the microphone? The loudspeaker? Could he see my copy of the *Police Almanac*? These and many other mystifying questions were rattled out in short gruff barks faster than machine-gun fire or so it seemed to me at the time. At long last when my head reeled with the effort of answering each bark before he barked again, my inquisitor's grim expression relaxed into warmth. 'You are all right!' he said and held out his hand like someone in an old movie about the upper classes. We shook hands, and he introduced himself as Colonel Geoffrey White, Chief Constable of Warwickshire, and thanked me for a most interesting experience.

Privately I thought the colonel's experience had been something more than merely interesting, but years of mediumship had taught me that for the true sceptic it is positively a point of honour not to be impressed whatever evidence they may be given. As I stood at the front door watching the colonel's upright figure striding off down the street, I did not expect to see him again.

As it happened I was wrong, because some months later he telephoned me early one Sunday morning and asked if he could have a sitting right away. I explained I did not sit with anyone on Sunday and offered him an appointment later in the week. He said his stay in London was short and asked me to make an exception in his favour. I was so impressed by the urgency in his voice that I agreed to sit with him that morning.

Hardly had I switched off the light in the seance room when Mickey said that Colonel White's father wanted to talk to him about 'the new post in Cyprus'. A long talk ensued between the colonel and his father to which I had perforce to listen. It appeared that Colonel White had been summoned to the Home Office on the previous Friday when he had been asked if he would accept being seconded to serve under the Colonial Office to undertake the re-organisation of the police force in Cyprus, then in the throes of its Graeco-Turkish troubles. The colonel was due to attend another interview at the Home Office on the following day when he would be expected to give his decision, and he was uncertain what that decision should be. His dead father told him with some vehemence he must accept the assignment because his particular capabilities were needed in Cyprus at this dangerous time. The father assured his son he would perform the task well and no harm would come to him while he was in the island. He added that the colonel would return home to England very much sooner than was at present thought possible. When I switched on the light after the voice had ceased, Colonel White was leaning back in his chair with an expression of stupefaction on his face. 'That was absolutely fantastic,' he said, 'not only am I utterly convinced that it was my father who was speaking to me but no one on earth apart from myself and the very important official I saw at the Home Office knew I had been asked to go to Cyprus. It is so highly confidential a mission that I haven't even told my wife yet!'

The colonel duly went to Cyprus and having done the work he had been sent to do, came home safe and sound far sooner than had been anticipated. Once he was back in England Colonel White made a point of sitting with me whenever he was in London, until one day I read in my daily paper he had suffered some kind of seizure as he rose to make a speech at a police banquet and had died instantly. I like to think that his father was there to welcome him on the other side.

Atheists and some members of Christian orthodoxies, especially those who have never sat with a medium of any kind, often ridicule the guides who help mediums to act as bridges between this world and the next. Red Indians? Ancient Egyptians? Tibetan Lamas? Children? How deluded and ridiculous can these Spiritualists get? Scoffers with pretensions in the field of psychology talk knowingly about secondary personalities, fragmented consciousness, subconscious dramatisation and auto-hypnotic phenomena. I do not pretend to know what they mean and I doubt if they know either. Some believers in the more rigid of the orthodoxies do not hesitate to denounce our guides and communicators as evil and personating spirits seemingly unmindful of the Psalmist who said, 'For he shall give his angels charge over thee to keep thee in all thy ways.' Of course I know some Christians accept the concept of guardian angels but because religious art has visualised them as Caucasian supermen improbably equipped with wings, one might be forgiven for supposing spiritual evolution to be a prerogative of the white race. The truth is simpler and more wonderful. Angels, guides, spirit helpers, call them what you like were once men and women of all races and all creeds who lived on earth and now, from whatever plane of being they inhabit they continue to evolve spiritually by trying to help and uplift mankind through the physical organism of persons on earth who have psychic gifts of one kind or another. Not only psychics have spirit helpers of course, to paraphrase St Paul, 'we are all compassed about with a great cloud of witnesses', which does not mean that a host of prying spirits hang around to observe our every action, however private, but simply that those we love who have gone before, care for us still and draw near us when we think of them with longing or send out a prayer for help.

During the war my spirit helpers were joined by another who introduced himself at my home circle as Dr Marshall who once lived and practised medicine in Hampstead, London. The personality which his warm sympathetic voice suggested was that of everyone's ideal family doctor. From snippets of information Dr Marshall gave us about himself from time to time we were able to verify some facts about his life on earth. Dr Charles Frederick Marshall was born in Birmingham in 1864 and received his medical training at Bart's Hospital in London where he gained a reputation for brilliance in both medicine and surgery. He was interested in psychical research when the subject was still considered cranky and eventually he became a convinced Spiritualist. Originally he specialised in diseases of the skin but later he turned to research in cancer. After years of this study he believed he had discovered a new approach to the disease and a new method of treatment. In 1932 he published *A New Theory of Cancer* in which he propounded his theories and described a number of advanced cases which he claimed had been cured by his method. Unfortunately, the medical pundits were not interested and he died a disappointed man in May 1939. Since he first came, Dr Marshall has advised and helped literally thousands of my sitters about their health or emotional anxieties.

My good friends Mr and Mrs Archer came to sit with me

one day, accompanied by Roland, a son of twenty who was in the Merchant Navy. I noticed one of Roland's eyes was swollen, bloodshot and watering profusely and asked him what was wrong. He told me the eye had been giving him pain and discomfort for months but none of the doctors he had seen had been able to find the cause of the trouble. It was obvious the young man was worried and not less so because he had recently been seen by an eminent ophthalmic specialist who had also failed to find any reason for the symptoms. During the seance Dr Marshall came to speak to the Archers and immediately he touched on the subject of Roland's eye. He reminded the young man of an occasion some months before when he had been cleaning portholes with a bundle of steel wool and told him that a minute particle of the steel wool had broken off and lodged in his eye and it was this which was causing the pain and irritation. He advised Roland to go back to the Eye Hospital and tactfully to suggest to the eminent specialist this possibility. The boy took Dr Marshall's advice and the particle of steel wool was duly located and surgically removed.

I began to look forward more and more to my sittings with George Woods and Betty Greene. The entities who came to speak to them were so various and so interesting. Some were famous during their time on earth, others had lived in obscurity, but all of them had something interesting, informative or uplifting to say which was recorded on tape so that George and Betty could share their sittings with all who cared to listen. At one of their sessions a spirit with a marked French accent introduced himself as Richet and, in the course of conversation with him, we learned he was the late Professor Charles Richet, the eminent French physiologist who in 1905 was President of the Society for Psychical Research in London. He explained to me how my mediumship was used by those on the other side. He said that every living being has a substance known as ectoplasm which is a life force, and, a physical medium like myself has a great deal more of it than

most people. During a seance this substance, which is sometimes also referred to as 'the power' is drawn from the
medium and fashioned by spirits who understand such matters
into a replica of the physical vocal organs which is known as
the 'voice-box' or sometimes 'the mask'. The communicating
spirit then concentrates his or her thoughts into this voice-box
and in doing so creates a frequency or vibration which reaches
the sitters on earth as objective sound. The late professor
went on to speak of the difficulties of this means of communication from the spirit's point of view. He told us that not only
must the communicating entity lower his own frequency to
the lower one of earth but simultaneously he must remember
what his voice sounded like in his lifetime and recapture
memories of happenings which will give proof of his identity
to the person with whom he wishes to communicate. When
the professor was asked by a sitter whether he could see and
hear people at a seance he answered that it depended on the
amount of concentration he put into the effort to do so. If he
focused his mind sufficiently he could both hear and see
people on earth but he found it simpler to apprehend their
thoughts before they were uttered as words. He grew quite
testy when someone suggested that sometimes the voices of
communicators from the spirit world did not sound exactly
the same as their voices during their life and he said it was
hardly likely they would sound the same, seeing they were not
using the same vocal organs they had in life. He added that we
must take into account, also, that the communicating spirit
was trying to concentrate on three different things at the same
time while communicating. Most of what Richet said made
sense to me. I had often heard communicators remark on the
difficulty of 'speaking through this box thing which wobbles
about all the time', or say plaintively how confusing it was to
remember some event which would prove beyond doubt who
they were while concentrating so hard on other things. As the
discarnate Professor Richet remarked rather grumpily: 'The
miracle is that we can communicate at all.'

Although some communicators speak in what I think of as standardised voices, by which I mean one elderly gentleman may sound much the same as another of similar educational level and young officers killed in the last war tend to speak in voices which resemble one another; it is what the entities say and the personality the voices express, together with the evidence they give which establishes identity to those with whom they seek to communicate. Some spirits, however, perhaps because of their superior mental powers, manage to reproduce voices which are unmistakably those which they had during their earth lives and one of them was Lord Birkenhead, a former Lord Chancellor of England who died in 1930.

Under the Homicide Act of 1957 five categories of murder were punishable by hanging and at a seance I held during the period when this Act was law, Lord Birkenhead manifested in my seance room and spoke eloquently and urgently for almost an hour on the necessity for total abolition of the death penalty. When he had introduced himself simply as Birkenhead, he said: 'This is an aspect of criminal law most in need of change; whether it is through the hangman's noose or whether it is done by some other supposedly more humane method nothing justifies the taking of life outside the law or inside it.'

Admitting the views he now expressed were quite opposed to those he held on earth he explained this by saying: 'I have seen the effects on this side of life when the law sends here souls who are unprepared and unready, their minds in turmoil, filled with thoughts of hate, revenge and fear. These souls linger near the earth,' he went on, 'and often what are known as carbon-copy murders are due to such earthbound revengeful entities who impinge their thoughts on individuals in your world who may already be mentally unstable and cause them to commit the same kind of crime for which the entity forfeited his life under the law.' As an alternative to capital punishment Birkenhead suggested, 'the unfortunate people who commit murder could be put to useful work, they should be made to serve society in some way and given the opportunity to work out their own salvation and repentance.' Towards the end of his impressive speech he declared: 'There is no death. We live and we try constantly to inspire you. I ask you, I beg of you, I plead with you to do all in your power to bring this truth to all humanity.'

When a recording of this communication by the former Lord Birkenhead was played to Mr Charles E. Loseby, M.C., Q.C., he said: 'It is Birkenhead all right. There is not a shred of doubt in my mind. As Birkenhead was responsible for my being called to the Bar I knew him particularly well during virtually the whole of his legal career.' Mr Loseby was later interviewed on television and repeated this statement in front of millions of viewers. When I heard he had done so I remembered Ellen Terry's promise which at the time had seemed so impossible of fulfilment.

Lilian Baylis, the indomitable woman who took over a derelict theatre and transformed it into the world-famous Old Vic, unexpectedly made a dramatic speech at a seance I held two days after the curtain had been rung down at her theatre for the last time to make way for the National Theatre. Miss Baylis expressed chagrin that the 'Vic' had not been retained as a training school for stage aspirants and asked if it were really necessary to lose a name which had for so long upheld English drama. 'Surely it could have been kept as a memorial to the past,' she said sadly. When one of the sitters asked if she had been present at the last performance in her theatre, Miss Baylis answered with a trace of impatience: 'Of *course* I was there! Do you think I would be missing for the last act? It was a sad night but for me a proud one. I am sure the National Theatre must be a success because its roots were in the Old Vic and those roots were strong.' Miss Baylis told us many other famous theatrical figures of the past were also present on the farewell night, including her aunt Emma Cons who years before had run the Old Vic as a people's theatre.

When the recording of Lilian Baylis' dramatic talk at this

seance was played to Captain P. Newcombe of Hove, he wrote as follows: 'The tape recording did quite certainly bring before us an exact picture of the late Miss Baylis as I remember her, the voice and mannerisms were unmistakable. I am most grateful for the opportunity of hearing my dear old friend once again.'

Mrs A. Watson, who also lives in Hove, is a god-daughter of the late Lilian Baylis and when she heard the recording she wrote: 'I am only too happy to confirm that it was Lilian Baylis' voice I heard which I am sure it is.'

I was visiting friends one evening and while we sat chatting about this and that I began to feel a strong personality impinging on me psychically and, though I tried to ignore this awareness, eventually it became too strong to resist and I suggested to my friends that if they drew the curtains and put out the light we might find out who this personality was. The curtains were drawn and the light put out, but only partial darkness was possible because of the impromptu nature of the sitting. Fortunately they had a tape-recorder. The incomplete black-out did not stop the personality whose presence I had sensed from speaking almost immediately in a strong voice with a decided Irish lilt. At first none of us knew who it was but when he mentioned his plays and said that despite their success he had no desire to return to earth again because to have been G.B.S. was experience enough for any man, we greeted him with delight. In his lifetime Shaw had always expressed disbelief in a life beyond the grave and a lady present asked him what was his reaction when he died and found he had been mistaken. He answered, 'I was very much surprised and very much perturbed but at the same time elated if one can have three such different emotions at once.' One of my friends tried to get him to criticise the theatre of today but he refused, saying he never now condemned because he had learned it was a sin. 'I have never been terribly keen to be a sinner,' he added, 'when I tried I was never very successful, much to my disappointment, I wanted to sin once or twice with two charming ladies but they would not sin by correspondence. I was a very sentimental old fool but I would not have people know it, I tried to hide it and put on a brusque manner, waggling my beard to frighten people, but I think I was more successful with my pen than I ever was with my tongue.' After talking to us for some time Shaw indulged in some self-criticism. 'Some of my characters were just puppets to express my own ideas and I admit that a couple of my plays are quite "unactable" but I like to think I created one or two characters which will live.'

When this tape recording was played to L. F. Easterbrook, O.B.E., in 1962, he wrote: 'I found the G.B.S. recording interesting indeed. The more I think about it, the more impossible it seems for anyone but himself to have been responsible. It brought back to me the sense of infectious gaiety you got with him when he was in the family circle and not showing off. You felt the world with all its follies was tremendous fun, to be laughed at with gentleness and understanding.'

Concerning the same recording the Rev. W. A. B. Barham wrote in June 1970, 'In March 1959 I played the G.B.S. tape to George Bishop, dramatic critic of the *Daily Telegraph*, and a close friend of Shaw for many years. After Mr Bishop had listened to the tape, he declared, "The mind and the mood are Shaw's." '

By no means all the personalities who came to speak to George and Betty at their regular sittings were well known in life, men and women who had lived and died quite unremarkably also came to talk about themselves, and tell us how they died and what they found on the other side of death. There was Edward Butler for instance who invited us to call him Ted in a warm Yorkshire accent. He told us he had lived in Leeds until a Saturday morning in 1923 when he went shopping with his wife. As he put it himself: 'I was crossing the High Street and before you could say Jack Robinson something hit me. It was a lorry and it got me pinned against the wall and I was out.' Then he told us he saw a crowd looking down at something so he went to have a look, to his surprise he saw a man on the ground who looked like him. 'I didn't realise it was me at first,' he said, 'I thought that's a rum do, he could be my twin brother. I didn't cotton on it *was* me!' Ted saw his wife in the crowd, crying, he tried to tell her he was all right but she ignored him completely. When the ambulance arrived Ted got inside with his wife and the body, and during the ride to the mortuary he 'cottoned on' at last. Later Ted went to his funeral and about this, he said: 'I thought to meself at the time all this fuss and how d'you do and expense for nothing because there I was in the carriage with the wife and nobody took any notice of me.'

According to his own account Ted had been a material kind of chap, he had given no thought to religion and had no belief in an after life. It seems he was earthbound for a time. He hung about his own home, travelled on tramcars, visited the homes of friends but no one could see him or hear him and he began to be lonely and unhappy. Sometimes he even longed for a glass of beer but though he felt solid to himself when he tried to pick up a glass his hand went right through it.

At another sitting an entity who spoke with a guttural German accent told us his name in life had been Dr Franck and he had been a prisoner in Dachau concentration camp where he had been killed because he refused 'to do certain things they want me to do which I not like'.

When he was first sent to Dachau Dr Franck had been allowed to use his medical skill to help other prisoners and he found life in the camp bearable, but later on 'they' had insisted he co-operate in some of the horrific surgical experiments performed on the inmates and when he refused he was executed. He told us that round Dachau even today there hangs an atmosphere of misery, unhappiness and evil because of the things which were done there. When Dr Franck was asked about his life on the other side he told us he was still a doctor but now he treated souls by helping them to rid themselves of old stagnant ideas, fear, hatred and prejudices which impeded their spiritual progress. Before he left us Dr Franck said: 'People on earth ought to realise that as a man thinks so he is, and by his thoughts and actions on your side of life so he creates his own heaven or his own hell over here.'

In 1963 the Profumo scandal shook the country and Stephen Ward, a fashionable osteopath and an artist of some talent, stood trial at the Old Bailey on charges arising from the affair. While he was still on bail and before verdict or sentence could be pronounced Ward took his own life. I had never met Stephen Ward nor any of his intimates, the social levels on which we moved were too disparate for that and I knew nothing of him apart from what I had read or heard from the mass media. I was therefore all the more surprised when soon after his lonely and pitiful death Stephen Ward was brought to speak in my home circle. In a hoarse, strained whisper Ward said he regretted the manner of his passing but his conscience was clear regarding the crimes of which society had accused him. 'I made mistakes, I was vain and very foolish, but I did not do the things they said I did and I ought to have stuck it out to the end.'

Not long after this first difficult communication, Stephen Ward returned to speak to my circle and this time his voice was stronger and he was able to talk for a longer period. Again he expressed regret for 'throwing in his hand' but he said he had felt a net of lies closing in on him, pointing to his guilt when he was innocent of anything but folly and a snobbish desire to be in the swim. He told us he had kept his mouth shut to protect the very people through whose fault he was in the dock and they had deserted and betrayed him. 'It was a dirty business,' he said, 'I was the scapegoat in an affair which was basically political, but behind it was something more sinister.' He said his suicide had not solved his problems but had made them harder to bear and spoke about some writings he had left behind for publication. He seemed to think these would be suppressed in England but might be published in another country before long. In fact I believe some writings by Stephen Ward were published in France soon after this sitting. Ward continues to speak in my home circle from time to time and I can report he has progressed spiritually to the point where he has forgiven himself for 'not sticking it out' and he no longer bears any resentment towards the friends who deserted him in his hour of need.

Ethel and Alfred Scarfe who live in Ipswich had been sitting with me for some time and sending out recordings of their seances to inquirers in the same way as George Woods and Betty Greene had been doing for so long. In January 1964 Mr and Mrs Scarfe were contacted by an evolved soul who told them he was once a member of the Catholic Church and a monk in a great monastery in the place we now call Bury St Edmunds. He told them to call him Brother Boniface and described himself as 'something of a rebel' in his day. From that time Brother Boniface has spoken with the Scarfes on many occasions and always with a fluency and a beauty of phraseology at which I can only marvel. He discourses on all kinds of moral questions and one of his recurrent themes is the evil folly of discrimination on grounds of race, colour, class or creed. Mr and Mrs Scarfe have sent many of his discourses on this theme to South Africa and letters constantly come from there asking for more copies.

On one occasion I played a recording of one of Brother Boniface's discourses to the pastor of a West End Church. He listened with interest and then asked if he might borrow the tape to play to one or two friends. Gladly I agreed to lend it to him. Some time afterwards another friend of mine who is a member of the pastor's fashionable congregation reported to me that the pastor had delivered Brother Boniface's discourse practically verbatim as his Sunday sermon, but needless to say he had not mentioned his source.

By the beginning of 1970 George and Betty had built up a library of more than 200 tape-recordings of spirit communications. The communicators speak in all manner of accents and dialects and though many were famous during their lives on earth, others were ordinary men and women who returned to tell us of their experiences when they died and what they found when they reached life's other side.

There is one recording among this comprehensive collection which had puzzled us for some long time. At the seance when it was taken Mickey announced he was bringing two people who had lived in ancient times to speak to George and Betty. Thereafter a male and a female voice were heard talking together in some unknown tongue. After a time the woman sang several little ditties. We still hope that one day we will find someone who will not only be able to identify the language but to translate the recording into English.

I had been living and working quietly and obscurely for close on eighteen years when without warning one Sunday I opened a newspaper to find a double page spread on my work with George and Betty. A further article on the following Sunday concluded, 'This was an extraordinary case with evidence to suggest a conscious life after death.'

As a result of this unsought publicity I was invited to be interviewed on television. Some recordings of spirit voices taken by George and Betty at their sittings were played during the programme, one of them fittingly that of Ellen Terry, and I did my best to expound the truth as I know it to the millions of people watching.

Fourteen

WHEN my old friend Father Sharp died in 1960 he was 94 years of age, but he had never ceased to hope that one day the brave dream of The Confraternity would become a reality and Spiritualism would be brought within the framework of the Established Church. One of the most grievous disappointments of his life was the suppression by the then Archbishop of Canterbury of the Report on Spiritualism produced by a Commission of churchmen who had spent many months investigating its claims. This Commission had been set up by the late Dr Cosmo Lang when he was Archbishop of York, but when he became Primate of England he suppressed the findings of his own Commission which by a majority verdict reached the conclusion that the claims of Spiritualism to communicate with the dead through specially gifted persons were true.

Lord Lang died in 1945 and one year later he spoke to Father Sharp in our home circle through my mediumship. This is what he had to say: 'If only I could have my life over again with the knowledge I now have, how differently I would act. I could have done so much, but I was afraid.' He went on to speak of the thousands of young souls precipitated into the next world by the war who were resentful because the Church had not taught them that death is not the end and a bridge can be made between the two worlds.

Cosmo Lang spoke on another occasion in my seance room when George Woods and Betty Greene were the sitters. In 1959 this is what he said: 'I feel strongly that Spiritualism is so vital and so important that all should know it, but I feel also that it is dangerous if it is used in the wrong way. I think it is important that colleges or societies should be organised where mediums could be sheltered and fed while they are trained in a proper manner to make their mediumship a vocation in the same way as does one who goes into the ministry, giving up his whole life to it, setting himself apart from the world, yet of the world and serving it. If you are to contact the highest forces, the good forces, those who can uplift mankind, you must have mediums or instruments who are of like mind and of like thought and on a higher spiritual vibration, and it seems to me some of your mediums are unfortunately of a low order. I do not want you to think I condemn, far from it, I am anxious to help. I feel that only when Spiritualism is used in the right way with mediums on a higher mental and spiritual level who will give up material things in true service to God, regarding themselves as mere instruments of the divine power to serve the children of the Earth, will it be of true benefit to mankind. It seems to me that while you are, as it were, only scratching the surface of the astral worlds which ninety per cent of your instruments seem to be doing, then Spiritualism is not only bad, it can even be dangerous, because like can attract like. Low entities who cling to your Earth can use mediums and through them tell people of things which are not true and which may be the cause of much unhappiness and misery. More dangerous still, the outcome of such seances may be that you can be obsessed by low entities who will distort you and distort truth. It is so important that when you sit you must choose your instrument carefully and conduct yourself in the right way. That you should first approach God not only when you pray but in your lives by endeavouring to make them a living prayer in both thought and action.' The former Primate went on to say how far adrift the Church of today had gone from its original teachings and its original force for good and how it had strayed from the simple path that Jesus had prepared. He said much of the teaching of Spiritualism was the *essence* of the Early Church, those Christians who gathered together and were possessed of the power of the Lord and who overcame the flesh and gave up all to follow Jesus. He concluded: 'If the great truth of survival were demonstrated and made manifest in the truest and finest sense, the whole world could be changed for the better.'

A recording of this communication from Cosmo Lang was played at the London Conference of the Churches' Fellowship for Psychical and Spiritual Studies in September 1960 and much discussion followed among members who had known Dr Lang during his lifetime. In 1965 George Woods received the following letter from the late Conan Shaw, the notable psychical researcher and writer:

Dear Mr Woods,

Tape Recording of Dr Cosmo Lang (the late Archbishop of York) 1 October 1960, through the Independent Direct Voice. Medium: Mr Leslie Flint. After hearing and studying this tape I should like to place the following on record:

As a chorister in York Minster (1908–15) I had many opportunities of coming into direct contact with Dr Lang. On a number of special occasions I was chosen to carry the Archbishop's train. Dr Lang used to row us choristers in a boat on the River Ouse from Bishopthorpe Palace. His slow style of speech comes out well on the tape as do his mannerisms. Both hands would clasp the top of his stole, then he would build up to a climax on one word or one phrase as he does on the tape to the word NOW and the phrase 'then shall they stand up in the Church and proclaim it' (this refers to Communication). His head would turn left to right, then right to left and centre observantly getting his three points home to the whole congregation.

Yes, I have every confidence it is Dr Cosmo Lang who is the communicator as he claims to be on the tape.

(signed) Conan Shaw

The former Lord Lang's critical remarks about mediumship today are not without foundation. In recent years Spiritualism has come to rely more and more on mental mediumship to prove its case and though there have been many wonderful clairvoyants, clairaudients and trance mediums in the past, today's mental mediumship, with a few notable exceptions, is not of a high standard. Except possibly in the privacy of home circles physical mediumship like my own gift of independent direct voice or the gift of materialisation whereby spirits can materialise into forms recognisably their own in life, solid to the touch and capable of speech, is practically non-existent. For this I blame the times we live in and the tempo at which we live our lives. Physical mediumship is an inborn gift but it takes a long time and much patience to bring it to its full development, in my case it took seven years of sitting in a dedicated circle regularly and without fail to bring my gift to its fruition. The rush and bustle of today with its demand for instant success, instant results, instant mediumship cannot produce the great mediums both mental and physical who were available to researchers in more leisurely times when intellectual giants like Professor William Barrett, Sir William Crookes, Frederick Myers, Sir Oliver Lodge and others of like eminence were able to experiment with them and finally reach conviction that human personality survives bodily death. It is a sad and sobering thought that there has probably never been a time when this knowledge has been more sorely needed. All round us we see the breaking down of moral values, the failure of authority, stagnation in the Churches and the impoverishment of family life and our youth, rebellious and searching, is driven to a false chemical perception of something 'other' which the hallucinogen drugs can give momentarily and at such damaging cost. And yet, among these forlorn and deceived children there may be many potentially great mediums whose gifts will never develop because there are now so few of us who can give them conviction and show them the way.

In August 1967 the former Cosmo Lang spoke again, this time in my own home circle, and I would like to quote an excerpt from the tape recording we made of his discourse. He said: 'The study of the human race from time immemorial is in itself an object lesson to all, yet we heed not the lessons we have learned, we do not see the present in the past, but what is the present but the result of past events, past mistakes, past foolishness? Man has turned his back for centuries upon truth and he does not see that there within himself in his innermost soul is the paramount truth of all, the indestructible truth that man is truly Spirit and thus immortal. Often I think back to my early years and how with enthusiasm I did step out on the path of religious instruction and experience. How often I spoke from the pulpit to the many who had gathered to listen to the word of God, and I strove to give out truth as I saw it and as I felt I knew it. As I look back, I see what I lacked was simplicity and knowledge of the power of the Spirit within. If only I had seen what underlay the teachings not only of Jesus but of many of the Prophets and the great reformers and teachers of earlier times. If I could only have seen the golden thread which runs from earliest times through all the great religions and realised that that single thread is the basis of all truth, that all men are of the Spirit and part of the great plan and that all life no matter what form it takes is indestructible and that even the lowliest creatures on earth have their place and their purpose not only in your world but also in ours. Man so often thinks of Spirit as having shape or form or as a glory to come after death, but Spirit is none of these things. It is the force which animates all who live in human form, everything in nature, and all manifestations of life in the universe. It is the force, the power, the vibration of life and because all life is part of the same Spirit it is indestructible. While you live on earth you are on the same wave-length, vibration or frequency as all around you and thus your physical senses perceive your surroundings as real and solid. But science has told you that nothing on earth *is* real or solid, the chairs you are sitting on now seem solid to you but in reality they are open networks of electrical charges whirling around a central nucleus at a frequency which is the same as your own. When you die you will continue to live in your more subtle spiritual double which is often called the astral body and which vibrates at a greater frequency than does your physical body. This astral body is on the same wave-length as the plane of being you will inhabit after death and for this reason everything in that plane will seem to you as real and as solid as once your earth surroundings appeared to be.'

Sometimes the astral body is projected from its physical sheath during a person's lifetime. This projection can happen involuntarily as the result of a shock, or under anaesthesia, or under hypnosis, but some persons master the technique of projecting at will. Those who have had the experience of find-ing themselves 'out' in another body say that the body in which they are separate is connected with their physical one by a pulsating cord of silver light which elongates as the 'double' moves away from the physical form They say they can see their other body lying inert wherever the projection occurred, on a bed, a couch, or even sitting in a chair. Sometimes they report a feeling of great reluctance to return to the physical body because they feel so light and joyous in the 'double'. While 'out' they find no difficulty in walking through walls and merely by thinking of where they want to be they find themselves there. Some who have had the experience have de-scribed how, when they tried to pick up material objects, they found that their hands went right through whatever object they tried to lift. This, if you remember, was the experience of Ted Butler the communicator who described to us his days as an earthbound spirit. The majority of people who report these experiences not only stress the joyousness of being 'out of the body' but they say they are convinced the spiritual counterpart in which they found themselves is the form in which they will continue to live after they die. I am told that psychiatry has another and more mundane explanation of this separation experience. I do not know what it may be, nor is it likely I would understand it if I were told, but if any psychiatrist has humility enough to learn from the Bible perhaps this quotation from Ecclesiastes 12, verses 6–7, may give him food for thought. 'Or ever the silver cord be loosed, or the golden bowl be broken ... then shall the dust return to the earth as it was, and the spirit shall return to God who gave it.'

On rare occasions it has happened that a living person has spoken in my seance room through my mediumship and when the sitter has exclaimed in wonder that this aunt or cousin or friend is still on earth the voice, usually a weak whisper, has faded. When the sitter, at my request, has checked up on the living communicator it has been found that the communicator was either ill and in coma, or deeply asleep at the time of the attempted manifestation. The conclusion seems irresistible that it was the spiritual counterpart, astral body or ectoplasmic double which made the communication while the physical body was unconscious and unaware.

When as happened recently the tenants of a council dwelling were re-housed on the grounds that their previous home was troubled by a poltergeist I think we can say the poltergeist has been given official recognition. Poltergeist phenomena, lights which switch themselves on and off, crockery which sails through the air or smashes itself, weird noises and other more frightening manifestations are generally ascribed by the afflicted family to the presence of ill-intentioned spirits. Sometimes the rite of exorcism is performed in such disturbed homes, but thereafter the poltergeist obstinately continues to make life intolerable for the unfortunate occupants. It has been observed by those who investigate phenomena of this kind that the disturbances tend to occur in the vicinity of a boy or a girl at or near the age of puberty. If fraud, prankishness or any physical cause for the occurrences can definitely be excluded then in my opinion it is likely that the youngster around whom the activity centres may be one of those people like myself who are born with an overplus of ectoplasmic power, but because of the young person's inexperience and lack of knowledge of this power within himself entities from lower planes of the next world can use the potential mediumship to manifest in an irresponsible and mischievous way. In view of the almost complete lack of physical mediumship today it is my opinion that if such young persons are found they should be made the subject of careful and responsible study and thereafter the mediumship should be developed along the highest ethical and spiritual lines.

People living in houses haunted by some apparition often seek the help of an exorcist to get rid of their unwanted guest, but this is not always the best nor the kindest way to clear a haunted house. Exorcism, with its opening volley of 'Retro me, Sathanas!' presupposes the entity is an evil one whereas it may be simply a lonely and unhappy earthbound soul. The kinder way is to procure the services of a medium, preferably accompanied by his home circle. Whether the medium is clairvoyant, clairaudient or a trance-control subject is not important because the entity can be contacted by any one of these psychic gifts. Once the contact is made the medium and his friends can find out why the spirit is tied to the place where it wanders and by offering their sympathy and their prayers they can persuade the restless soul to cease troubling the home of others and depart to seek its own place on the next plane of existence. This service to the dead is known as rescue work and many home circles devote their weekly meetings to work of this kind.

There is another kind of haunt where a spectral figure or figures will pointlessly and endlessly re-enact some scene from the past in the place where it originally occurred. The scene is always one which at the time must have generated strong emotions and desperate thoughts, a murder or a suicide or something of the sort. The spectres who endlessly re-enact this scene are not necessarily the spirits of those who originally participated in it. Emotions and thoughts which are strong enough can be registered on the atmosphere of the place where the happening originally occurred and someone with a psychic faculty of which he may even be unaware can for a fleeting moment of time re-activate these thoughts and emotions and witness the scene which gave rise to them. We know so little about time but I imagine there is some parallel to be drawn from radio and television today. If our receivers are sensitive enough and tuned to the proper vibration or frequency then they can pick up and register from the atmosphere the words and actions of people who are half the world away and convey them to us as the very moment at which they are happening. It seems to me a not impossible hope that one day our scientists may discover the wave-length, frequency or vibration on which the next plane of being operates and when they do communication between the two worlds could become a fact of every-day life.

On 16 June 1969 some weeks before the American astronauts landed on the moon an entity, who gave his name as John Grant, predicted that the landing would be successful and that the men involved would return safely.

One of the happier events in the life of a medium is when his mediumship is used to confirm the mediumship of another. I had this privilege recently when Rosemary Brown, the music medium through whom various dead composers, Liszt, Chopin, Busoni, Beethoven and others give new compositions to the world, came to sit with me. Almost as soon as I turned off the light Sir Henry Wood announced himself as 'compère' of the seance. Sir Henry brought many of Rosemary's musical inspirers to speak to her, including Chopin, who said of her: 'The group of musicians in spirit chose Rosemary because of her simplicity, if they had communicated through an accomplished musician the experts would have questioned this proof of man's survival of death!' He went on to say it was necessary to find someone ignorant to some extent, but 'you have great sensitivity and a love of music'. After the seance Rosemary said: 'If someone imitated a voice on the telephone it would eventually be recognisable as an imitation. I have no doubt these were the genuine voices of my musical directors as I know them through my own mediumship and what is more important, they made an impression of their individual personalities.'

I am often asked what my own feelings are during a seance. Am I fully conscious of what transpires? Do I in any way influence the phenomena? Do I ever go into trance during a seance?

I seldom go into trance unless the power is very weak and my spirit helpers want urgently to communicate for some good purpose. Usually I am very wide awake and I can hear all that is said both by my sitters and the spirit voices. Often I speak to the voices and I can converse with my own helpers and ask their advice about problems which vex me. There are recordings of seances where more than one spirit can be heard speaking at a time and sometimes I am heard to laugh or talk or cough when a spirit is speaking.

I have always been certain that my own vocal organs are never used for spirit communication and recently this was confirmed from an outside source by an expert in his field, William R. Bennett, Professor of Electrical Engineering at Columbia University in the City of New York. I first sat with Professor Bennett when he was in London in the summer of 1970 and subsequently had a number of pleasant meetings with him when I was myself visiting New York. The following statement by Profesor Bennett is quoted with his permission:

My experience with Mr Flint is first hand; I have heard the independent voices. Furthermore, modern investigation techniques not available in earlier tests corroborate previous conclusions by indicating that the voices are not his. But to be thorough, one should also consider the possibility of live accomplices, particularly when the seance takes place in the medium's home environment. This suggestion became untenable for me during his visit to New York in September 1970, when, in an impromptu seance in my apartment, the same voices not only appeared but took part in conversations with the guests. The logistics of transporting a concealed company of performers for this purpose appear to be too formidable for serious consideration.

As far as influencing the phenomena goes I am certainly unaware of ever being able to do so, though on very rare occasions I have mentally received some comment or remark a split second before a spirit voice utters it. I am of course clairvoyant also so I can often see as well as hear the spirit communicators, and sometimes when they are unable to get their voices through I may receive an evidential message for the sitter which may be some consolation for a poor sitting, but as a rule when the power is too weak for the voice communication to be possible, I and my sitters wait hopefully for a while then when nothing happens we give up the session.

Positively the only unusual feeling I have ever observed in myself is that sometimes I experience a feeling of intense cold during a seance even on a hot day when my sitters are grousing about the heat.

I have used my rare and strange gift as honestly, as selflessly and as devotedly as I have been able for thirty-five years now and my sixtieth birthday is almost here. I do not know how much longer I have left to serve and I am deeply concerned that I know of no one who can follow me. Perhaps I should end my story with an extract from a recording of a talk given by a spirit who gave his name only as 'Pierre'; he said:

Why is it that Spiritualism has not swept the whole world and changed the face of life in your world? It is because the average Spiritualist has not yet begun to realise what it means to be truly a Spiritualist in the real sense, to be prepared to give himself in love and in service to God, realising that the power which flows from Spirit can change not only himself but through him possibly the whole world. There are many different religions in your world, many confusing, conflicting ideas and thoughts, but there is one truth, and that is the truth of everlasting life, that all who die, live, and that those who come from this side of life and truly desire the welfare of mankind are concerned to find souls here and there who can be used as instruments in the highest sense. That is why we intend to protect this instrument, there are so few of his calibre and quality. We will protect this wonderful channel we have built over the years even against himself. People think a medium is like a machine, you put your money in the slot and automatically the machine works. It is not so. For any medium to sit all the time at the whim of this person or that person at the moment they desire it would be dangerous and futile, but we protect this medium more and more and not only do we expect him to do less and less, we intend to conserve his power so that it can be used only to obtain communications of value for the whole world.